FOOD FIGHT!

Latinx Pop Culture

SERIES EDITORS

Frederick Luis Aldama and Arturo J. Aldama

FOOD FIGHT!

Millennial Mestizaje Meets the Culinary Marketplace

Paloma Martinez-Cruz

THE UNIVERSITY OF
ARIZONA PRESS

TUCSON

The University of Arizona Press
www.uapress.arizona.edu

ISBN-13: 978-0-8165-3606-1 (paper)

Cover design by Leigh McDonald
Cover art: *Chili Queen* by Ute Simon

Publication of this book is made possible in part by the proceeds of a permanent
endowment created with the assistance of a Challenge Grant from the National
Endowment for the Humanities, a federal agency.

Library of Congress Cataloging-in-Publication Data
Names: Martinez-Cruz, Paloma, author.
Title: Food fight! : millennial mestizaje meets the culinary marketplace / Paloma
    Martinez-Cruz.
Other titles: Latinx pop culture.
Description: Tucson : The University of Arizona Press, 2019. | Series: Latinx pop
    culture | Includes bibliographical references and index.
Identifiers: LCCN 2018038446 | ISBN 9780816536061 (pbk. : alk. paper)
Subjects: LCSH: Cooking, Mexican—Social aspects—United States. | Cultural
    appropriation—United States. | Ethnic food industry—Social aspects—United
    States. | Decolonization—United States.
Classification: LCC HM621 .M3714 2019 | DDC 306.0973—dc23 LC record
    available at https://lccn.loc.gov/2018038446

Printed in the United States of America
♾ This paper meets the requirements of ANSI/NISO Z39.48-1992 (Permanence of
Paper).

This book is dedicated to the Fair Food Program, the Coalition of Immokalee Workers, and the dedicated network of crop workers and consumers that power the protection of our food and its producers.

CONTENTS

ILLUSTRATIONS

ACKNOWLEDGMENTS

A Zen contemplation recited before dining begins with, "First, seventy-two labors have brought us this food. We should know where it comes from." The invocation of seventy-two labors, a reference to the intricacies of monastic divisions of labor, acknowledges that the meal doesn't happen as if by magic, but that innumerable workers, including farmers, crop workers, packagers, distributers, truck drivers, grocers, cooks, servers, and dishwashers, were all intertwined in the life-giving phenomenon of a full meal. Just as Zen practitioners acknowledge the spectacular determination of countless individuals in getting food on the table, my book must begin by honoring the seventy-two hands that have made the following pages possible.

Fundamental support for my research endeavors came from the Department of Spanish and Portuguese at The Ohio State University, with department chairs (in order of appearance) Glenn Martinez, Eugenia Romero, Laura Podalsky, and vice-chair Ignacio Corona all helping to foster a total environment of respect and unflagging commitment to Latinx studies. Frederick Luis Aldama, Lisa Voigt, Ana Elena Puga, Anna Babel, Michelle Wibbelsman, Isis Barra McElroy, Pamela Espinosa Monteros, and John and Tiffany Grinstead have read, discussed, or closely sustained the work that follows. I'm grateful to the Center for Latin American Studies and the Latin American Section of the Department of Spanish and Portuguese at OSU that have fostered collegiality and dedicated inquiry. My gratitude also goes to the editor-in-chief Kristen Buckles and the editorial assistant Stacey Wujcik at the University of Arizona Press for the many-layered review process that took this manuscript from the lonely writer's hermitage to become part of a wider conversation.

The uncompromising creative and political acuity of the Pocha Nostra corps of Guillermo Gómez-Peña, Balitrónica Gómez, Saul García-López, and Emma Tramposch are central to my Pocha critical lens through which I view popular culture. Generous assistance, encouragement, and unwavering support came from a cast that includes, but is not limited to: Dominica Rice-Cisneros, Carlos Salomon, Shanna Lorenz, Inés Valdez, Christine Rabenold, Alyshia Gálvez, Ester

Hernandez, John Cruz, Daniel Gallegos and Anamaria Ayala Meneses, Aaron Michael Morales, Leslie Brown, Magali Mireles, Francesca Osuna, D. Marcela Ampudia Sjogreen, Joshua Truett, Jordan Chaney, Sensei Randall Ryotan Eiger, Enkyo Pat O'Hara Roshi, Jacob and Kristen Sundermeyer, Matthew and Kimberly Davis, John and Beth Rice, Elena Foulis, Rubén Castilla Herrera, Laura Rodriguez, Moriah Flagler, Nicholas Pasquarello, Bryan Ortiz, Lalo Alcaraz, the Jumping Bean Café, the Coalition of Immokalee Workers, Bottoms Up Coffee Co-op, No Hate Space Columbus, the courageous cohort of Gender and Power and Be the Street students and collaborators that populate the halls of Hagerty, and the community of Cruz, Viveros, and Mojica family members that keeps me going.

Thank you to my mother, Rosa Martinez, for her enduring love and support, and the example of the deep respect for food and ancestors that she has shared with me; to my late father Richard V. Cruz for never taking us to a fast-food chain restaurant; to my brother, Camilo Cruz, for his diversion program wisdom; to my son, Emiliano Vargas, for his bravery on the Midwest food tour; and to Greg and Noreen Hicks, DiaQuan King, Gibson Hicks, and Gabrielle Hicks: how fortunate I am to be a part of your space walk, exploring the universe together. Finally, my gratitude goes to Eric Hicks, who has been my all-seasons cut man and fellow pilgrim in the challenges and joys that go into the fight.

FOOD FIGHT!

INTRODUCTION

A Close Fight

The barbed courtesy of the Mexican restaurant server in Mexico City who offers preferential treatment to U.S. tourists over Mexican nationals; the Chicana chef at the Oakland farmers market who is met with a condescending air of surprise from her Anglo male fellow industry professional when he sees her buy organic produce (because he assumes the Chicana will sacrifice quality for a lower cost); the racial defamation and mocking tone of "Mexican" restaurants geared toward the Anglo customer base; the high-end Latin-tinged eateries with Anglo chefs who give the impression that the food, like the expanse of land according to the logic of Manifest Destiny, was something unattended or poorly handled that they "discovered" or "rescued" from actual Latinos; the photo galleries depicting indigenous and mestizo coffee laborers gleeful to provide products for elite consumers in the North: the fight for ethical choices in food production and consumption is always close. After all, as bipedal hominids, our bodies require that we eat every day, and in the complex cross currents of the global economy, we are also obliged to vote every day, either by investing—or divesting—in the products and businesses that rely on our patronage for survival. *Food Fight! Millennial Mestizaje Meets the Culinary Marketplace* submits that food provisioning constitutes an urgent entry point into the fight for the life chances, dignity, and economic agency of indigenous, mestizo, Chicano, Mexican, Latinx, and Latin American peoples by uncovering some of the hidden realities that impact our decision-making when we step up to the electoral urn of our daily diet.

Since the ensuing conversation is predicated on a clear understanding of how I am using the key terms dealing with both cultural identity (mestizaje) and social justice (fight), I'll start with the *Oxford English Dictionary*'s following definition of mestizaje:

1. Interbreeding and cultural intermixing of Spanish and American Indian people (originally in Mexico, and subsequently also in other parts of Latin America); miscegenation, racial and cultural intermixing.
2. The action or process of such racial and cultural intermixing. *rare*.
3. Latin American people of mixed American Spanish (especially Mexican) and American Indian parentage, considered collectively. *rare*.[1]

Since the term's 1940s debut in the *Hispanic American Historical Review*, the term's adequacy as a descriptor has been hotly contested. Faced with the challenge of coming up with a name for a wildly diverse group unbounded by either geography or genetics, my recourse to "mestizaje" is not a function of the need for a medical or forensic identification of individuals who are "part this" and "part that." Rather, the third entry in the list above gets at what I am doing with the implications of "mestizaje" throughout my book's chapters, not because it is an ideal choice, but because it provides greater ideological flexibility than the alternative choices of Chicano, Mexican, indigenous, Hispanic, Latinx, Mesoamerican, or Spanish American.

Here it must be noted that, with the exception of "Chicano" to which group members historically self-subscribe, the preceding terms are the direct result of the settler-colonial impetus to categorize indigenous peoples for the purpose of their control. An exonym is the name for a place or a culture that comes from outside the local language custom (the endonym). Given this superimposition of a name that did not originate from the language that it describes, peoples of Latin American extraction have long contested, and are likely to contest for perpetuity, the exonyms that result from colonial expediency rather than any expression of kin or clan generated by the group's members.

Given the present conversation is precipitated by the violent elimination of endonymous identifiers, for an accountable exploration of Latin American hybridity and its consequences to garner any sort of cohesion, we must repeatedly, and literally, "come to terms" with the disjunctions and contestations that each generation brings to counter the violence of exonymic self-identification. From the outside, this vacillating approach to naming and identity may seem capricious or excessive, as when the travels from "Latino," to "Latina/o," to "Latinx" on course proposals or administrative statements are met with snide or frustrated remarks, but this evolution is both the desired and inevitable result of the commitment to greater inclusivity coupled with the challenges of languaging identities previously silenced by European conquest, U.S. imperialism, and the far-reaching consequences of patriarchal ascendancy.

As I come to terms with mestizaje on a hemisphere plagued by "slave names," it is necessary to acknowledge that the exercise of identity construction based on "racial mixture" represents a kind of acquiescence to the colonial logics of racial containment: always "part" something—never whole. As such, there is no lack of scholars and observers who take issue with mestizaje as a unifying paradigm extending from the Spanish conquest of the Americas. As Sheila Contreras points out, many have roundly rejected mestizaje's overt message of racial democracy that obfuscates the realities of race-based pigmentocracy, as Latin American elites embrace mestizaje's utopian implications as a "whitening" veil for its African and indigenous subjects who are totally excluded by the national project.[2] In her study of mestizaje, Josefina Saldaña-Portillo points out that not just elites, but also subaltern activist agendas take issue with the formulations of mestizaje and indigenismo, as the modern Zapatista movement, notable for its 1994 insurrection in San Cristobal, Chiapas, and consisting of 99 percent indigenous participants, refuses to make claims to civil rights based on "Indianness," but insists on being seen and heard as "citizens of the nation."[3]

With its contemporary roots in the indigenist and "bronze race" tropes proffered by Mexican minister of education José Vasconcelos in his seminal essay "La raza cósmica" (1925), the creation of the "mixed" identity also imperils progressive prospects by first idealizing a precolonial indigeneity characterized by its temporal distance, glory, and unsuccessful resistance, and secondly by subscribing to what Rafael Pérez-Torres describes as a "teleology of progress," wherein the ethnic Indian is posited as a primitive biological ancestor of the more progressive (and desirable) mestizo.[4] And even though we can count on the scientific rejection of biologically determined notions of race, we must also observe the evident diversity of humans and grapple with concepts of difference that form the basis of institutional, cultural, and social partitions that favor European features to the detriment of populations emerging from more indigenous ancestry.[5] "Mixing," in other words, does not draw from diverse ancestry in equal ways, and the romanticized reinvention of "fallen" classical Mesoamerican mythologies, without the concurrent commitment to be in dialogue with contemporary indigenous struggles and their proposed taxonomies of identity and political participation, perpetuates the logic of colonial domination when absorbed uncritically as a model for unity.

Even with these problematic valences that resonate in the Latin American context, mestizaje speaks with an entirely different inflexion when it crosses the border. Chicano indigenismo, developed in part by the poet Alberto Urista (also known as Alurista) in his preamble for the Plan Espiritual de Aztlán (1969), proposes an oppositional geographic identity rooted in the historical primacy of mestizos in today's U.S. Southwest. The historical vestiges of Aztec languages and cultures in the Southwest provide a pre-Anglo, but also pre-Mexican and pre-Spanish, ancestral link to the land on which their legitimate residency is continually contested.[6] While the deterritorialization of mestizo peoples and centuries of colonial policies and practices have divorced many from knowledge of their indigenous ancestors, the reproduction of classic Mesoamerican mythology and anthropology has lent Chicano indigenismo a framework for spiritual alignment and cultural cohesion. Mestizaje, as the offshoot of Chicano indigenismo particular to the imprint of the U.S.-Mexico border, serves as a contestatory identity that privileges indigenous ancestry over Spanish contributions to Mexican and Central American cultures.

Close to twenty years after Alurista's recuperation of the mythopolitical homeland of Aztlán, Gloria Anzaldúa's *Borderlands / La frontera* (1987) expanded the notion of mestizaje to encompass a feminist, spiritual vision of productive disruption. In order to transform internalized colonization (racial self-hatred) into the valorization of indigenous ancestry, Anzaldúa posits that the many ambiguities that characterize bordered identities give rise to the "nueva mestiza," or the creative, psychic pathway born of the rupture from nationalist and patriarchal paradigms.[7] Anzaldúa describes an occult zone of both instability and completion as the Coatlicue state, where dualities give way to nonbinary spiritual terrains that resuscitate aspects of self that were undervalued or thrown away.

I see *oposición e insurrección*. I see the crack growing on the rock. I see the fine frenzy building. I see the heat of anger or rebellion or hope split open that rock, releasing *la Coatlicue*. And someone in me takes matters into our own hands, and eventual activity, my soul, my mind, my weaknesses and strengths. Mine. Ours. Not the heterosexual white man's or the colored man's or the state's or the culture's or the religion's or the parents'—just ours, mine.

And suddenly I feel everything rushing to a center, a nucleus. All the lost pieces of myself come flying from the deserts and the mountains and the valleys, magnetized toward that center. *Completa*.[8]

In the above, Anzaldúa makes the case for a Mesoamerican-informed, decentered subjectivity as the ultimate pathway to feminist, queer, mestiza self-acceptance. As an early voice in radical Chicana feminism, her foundational contribution is summarized by Edwina Barvosa, who writes, "Anzaldúa's conception of mestiza consciousness is an exceptional starting point for a detailed theoretical account of multiple identities because it has numerous commonalities with other important discussions of multiplicity, and combines these elements with novel insights that warrant further investigation and elaboration."[9]

An early Chicana critique of the unitary subject, the subsequent elaborations on mestizaje made by Chicana feminists have been linked to Anzaldúa's nueva mestiza on both spiritual and intellectual levels. Adapting and evolving Anzaldúa's theorization of mestiza consciousness, Chela Sandoval's "Mestizaje as Method: Feminists-of-Color Challenge the Canon" (1998) contributes a political organization for mobilizing oppositional forms of consciousness in order to move toward a more diverse and compassionate social order. She investigates Chicana models of feminism, including "Chicana liberalism" (socioeconomic parity), "Chicana insurgency" (radical personal and institutional change), and "cultural nationalism" (cultural continuity over feminist thought),[10] adding to these her development of "Chicana mestizaje," configured by Sandoval as the psyche's survival of cultural crossings that occasion what she refers to as "mestiza double consciousness."[11] Born of decolonial and antisexist U.S. histories, Sandoval's U.S. Third World feminism—a mestiza, borderlands feminism—provides the critical apparatus for recognition and interpretation of the politics and expressive cultures of Chicanas and mestizas in the United States.[12] In sum, Chicana mestizaje, as located by Anzaldúa and Sandoval, serves as an index for feminist, antihomophobic, prophetic, resilient, and radical conceptual models that are both critical of the destructive pathway of hyperconsumerism and the exclusion of peoples differentiated by gender, sexuality, race, class, nationality, ethnicity, and other categories of identity that mark subjects for national exclusion.

In the ensuing chapters, I am particularly interested in mestizaje as a category of mobilization and reclamation. Following Cristina Beltrán's assessment of Latinidad as a "site of permanent political contest," I will use the term "mestizo" as a Chicana feminist political category that acknowledges the shared experience of national rejection in the United States context, rather than the positivistic construal that has come to represent Latin American elitist voicings of the term.[13] Understanding the always-already-exonymic nature of the mestizo category, my intention is not to advocate for the fixity of mestizaje's meaning but rather to enter into an urgent conversation about the foodways pertaining to Chicano, Mexicano, Latinx, indigenous, Mesoamerican, and Latin American histories, peoples, traditions, and culinary contributions under the most pointed yet expansive rubric available to me at this time.

Along with mestizaje, the concepts of social justice and decoloniality arise out of a specific context. Following the contributions of Walter Mignolo and Aníbal Quijano, I define decolonial practices as those which interrogate or erode the project of Western capitalism in favor of communal access to resources, and supplant the monopoly of aesthetic priorities that secure Euro- and U.S.-centric management of the senses in favor of the inclusion of non-Western traditions and innovations. Quijano explains the coloniality of power as a global ordering of truth, whereby time and space are segmented along a racial axis that has endured beyond the original sixteenth-century geopolitical conquests, with racial and cultural features as a central criterion for the formation of political hierarchies.[14] Today, this axis of power speaks through the ideology of neoliberal globalization, by which capital now assumes the civilizing project once identified with the colonial superimposition of monarchy and Christianity. This is why pathways to social justice organized along increased communal access to resources represent a move in the direction of eroding the colonial project of Western neoliberalism: collective, emancipated individuals constitute a revolutionary population at odds with the colonial priorities that emphasize nation building and private accumulation. The food provisioning and dining experiences analyzed in my study demonstrate how the coloniality of power—the colonial mind—can be reconfigured and reimagined so that decolonial imaginaries and practices may emerge as its challenger.

As for the title's "millennial," it's important to clarify that this book does not pursue a journalistic notion of the stereotypical Millennial that followed Baby Boomers of the '40s and Gen Xers of the '70s. As a label, the term has come to evoke images of young adults living in their parents' suburban homes, simultaneously fused to multiple electronic devices and screens, debilitated by anxiety as their parents and schools of privilege insist they are marked for greatness while delaying forays into #adulting as long as possible. If I'm not investigating this generation's cultural proclivities that journalists so gleefully excoriate, I'm also not shooting for a definition of the Chicano version of the Millennial generation, which Louis McFarland describes as a transcultural, transnational combination of youth identities.

> This new millennial mestizaje varies along a number of axes, including geography, class, race, gender, sexual orientation, and religion. Thus, we can no longer say, as we once attempted to do during the Chicano Movement of the 1960s and 1970s, that there is one single way to be a Chican@: a politically conscious person of Mexican descent who grew up in the United States.[15]

In both the mainstream, journalistic taxonomies of Millennials and McFarland's observation about the new pluralisms surrounding Chicano identity, the point is to get at the truth regarding today's youth and their involvement in national and/or hemispheric political processes.

In contrast, my study makes use of the term "millennial"—with a lower case "m"—to discuss today's location of mestizaje as an anti-hegemonic framing device with which to deconstruct and decolonize our moment's dominant foodways. At the heart of *Food Fight!* is the notion that perspectives informed by mestiza consciousness related to systems of contemporary food provisioning can encourage not only greater sustainability but also increased dignity and social justice in our national and transnational foodscapes. That being said, I understand that there really is no way to discuss anything with the "millennial" modifier that doesn't intersect on some level with the "now more than ever" need for actions that will swing the pendulum during our moment of tremendous humanitarian and environmental crisis. Like John Belushi's iconic "food fight!" war cry in the 1978 National Lampoon film *Animal House*, mestizaje at the millennium finds us reaching for imperative exclamatories: Boycott Monsanto! Education not deportation! Dump Trump! Defend DACA! Hands up, don't shoot! Show me what America looks like! We're in a time of tremendous precarity, uncertain that our cries will be loud enough to shift political will but certain that the fight is worth waging: perhaps the only certainty our corner of the millennial condition will allow.

My study is indebted to many steady—yet urgent—voices that are sounding the wake-up call for Latinx studies to get in the food fight. Luz Calvo and Catriona Rueda Esquibel's recent *Decolonize Your Diet: Plant-Based Mexican-American Recipes for Health and Healing* (2015) promotes a diet rich in plants indigenous to the Americas (corn, beans, squash, greens, herbs, and seeds) with the argument that physical health and spiritual fulfillment cannot be achieved through the Standard American Diet (the SAD diet). Alyshia Gálvez's *Eating NAFTA: Trade and Food Policies and the Destruction of Mexico* (2018) interrogates the trade policies that privilege the SAD diet and render heritage foodways the exclusive privilege of the hipster class, while transnational Mexican households have synchronously witnessed exponentially higher rates of diet-related illnesses such as diabetes mellitus, ischemic heart disease, and chronic kidney disease. Gustavo Arellano's *Taco USA* (2012) provides a cultural history of Mexican cuisine in the United States, telling the broader story of Chicano contributions to the national foodscape, while extremely valuable contributions are made by Laura Pulido and Julie Guthman that address the heightened exposure of rural workers to the hazards of pesticides and other dangerous conditions associated with farm labor.[16] By bringing agricultural workers' rights, dietary dangers, and historically submerged perspectives into focus, this short list of representative researchers champions the potential of Latinx food studies to shape more healthy, informed, and ethical eating. Where my approach differs is in my analysis of cultural expression as it pertains to food production. Culture, listing often toward a corpus of achievements in art, literature, film, and drama, is defined here to include the applied arts of culinary craft, the imagery and messaging of food product and restaurant advertising, and the performativity of Latinx and mestizo identities in national food systems. By interrogating the social inequalities of U.S. and mestizo food chains through the lens of cultural analysis, my work attempts to discern the difference between the fight for ethical eating and the fads and fanfare around products and services that obstruct the pathway to more equitable and healthful options.

And let's be clear—the fight is close. The kitchen recipe, the coffee pot, the table grape: the weapons of disruption are always near.

Don't Bring a Gun to a Fork Fight

They say the pen is mightier than the sword, but when we metaphorically weaponize our dietary practices, we can embody resistance with every swoop of the fork. My chapters follow the contours of my own embodied and geographic journey through the places where I dined, drank, observed, and interviewed participants at all levels of food provisioning and consumption. Some of it was delicious, but plenty of it was tragic. Even so, this book is not to be read as a lament. As I've heard cultural scholar Greg Tate say about the violence experienced far too often by people of color at the hands of repressive regimes: nightmare is the beginning of responsibility.

In terms of my own background, which serves as an instrument of interpretation throughout this book, I am originally from Los Angeles, California, of mixed Mexican and Puerto Rican heritage. I lived in Mexico City and attended la Universidad Nacional Autónoma de México during one year of my undergraduate career, and return regularly for both professional and personal opportunities. My assessments of food preparation are based on my culture and experiences, and the fact that I now reside in Columbus, Ohio, a state whose Latino population was reported to be about 3.4 percent in 2014.[17] After spending most of my life in Latino-dominant cities and neighborhoods, the quest for Mexican food that was somewhat relatable was one of the steepest challenges in adapting to Midwest living outside of Chicago. Also, I have been a vegetarian since high school, which naturally influences my exploration and interpretation of menu items, and I do a lot of home cooking for family and friends that stems from a California-based interpretation of Mexican foodways.

It's probably also useful to understand that no one would mistake me for a Millennial, in the generational implications of this term: cell phones at the table make me frown; I've never texted "LOL"; I opened my first email account during my last months as a senior in college. At home, I was shaped by the "latchkey kid" phenomenon, which was the descriptor commonly used to describe Gen X youth who were home alone after school owing to the increase in divorce rates, higher maternal participation in labor outside of the home, and scant childcare options for working-class families. My brother and I ate a lot of prepared and processed food in front of a TV before our mother arrived home from work, but on Fridays and weekends we enjoyed it when she took us to eat at the many diverse types of restaurants that Los Angeles had to offer: Thai, Japanese, Italian, Mexican, Lebanese, Greek, Indian, and Chinese restaurants, along with Kosher delis and pioneering vegan cafés, were all on our small family's steady rotation of dinner destinations. We ate lobster with large, buttery tortillas in Ensenada and escargot once at a French bistro on a road trip to Sacramento, with many tuna fish sandwiches and boxes of neon-orange macaroni and cheese in between. My culinary mestizaje was not always a glamorous thing. Once, during the early grade-school years, our Mexican grandmother packed us refried bean and chorizo sandwiches on toasted raisin bread (I spilled chocolate milk on it before I "accidentally" dropped it on the ground), and sometimes chorizo breakfast on Dad's weekend would result in gristle fights, as we spit the chewy, inedible bits out and threw them at each other in an exchange of hysterical, bouncing ballistics. I bring an irreverent, pocha (*agringada*) mestiza set of gustatory preferences to this book that was shaped by a Generation X home life and a pragmatic view of the difference between what we aspire to eat and feed our loved ones and what actually happens at mealtimes.

Since the publication of my first monograph, *Women and Knowledge in Mesoamerica: From East L.A. to Anahuac* (University of Arizona Press, 2011), I've been interested in exploring the notion of food preparation as radical mestiza feminist epistemology: the revaluation of knowledge transmission traditionally identified as women's work that is both economically exploited and societally undervalued. My own journey to decolonize and depatriarchalize the construction and flow of knowledge in Mesoamerican and Chicana cultures began as my frustration with the paucity of indigenous and mestiza women's contributions to the philosophical and aesthetic currents that define hemispheric cultures, and I found myself prefacing talks about my book with a question about mestiza exclusion from the Western history of ideas by saying something along the lines of, "So they have their Plato and their Socrates, but what do we have? The nacho chip?" I think I said it enough times that I needed to start questioning how easy it was to evoke Mexican food items that are meant to sound like a joke. If my first monograph was a labor of love to decolonize the way we think about intellectual and spiritual authority and reclaim the contributions of our shamans, healers, and midwives, then this book is about unpacking the other part of my rhetorical question that I had fanned about on so many occasions: the highly visible, ever-present, popular, and extroverted products, packaging, and marketing discourses that sustain colonial logics in our foodways by attacking indigenous and mestizo life chances, dignity, and ecological stewardship.

Chapter 1, "Farmworker-to-Table Mexican: Decolonizing Haute Cuisine," addresses the problem of mainstream food networks that call for better quality and greater sustainability in our food chains without acknowledging the circumstances of agricultural workers who are the first to experience the perils of harmful farming practices. Alice Waters, the pioneering figure behind what is referred to as the farm-to-table movement, opened Chez Panisse in Berkeley, California, in 1971. Waters and her cohorts centered the restaurant's fare around locally sourced, seasonal foods, and advocated for a new sensibility that supported ecologically sound agriculture, local communities, and traditional ways of life. This "movement" led to a new vision in U.S. dining, so that local, craft, and organic foods have come to signify the forefront of a dietary scaffolding that is both ecologically and aesthetically committed. By historically situating the Chicano movement as a locus of environmental awareness in the outcry for safer conditions and pay for farmworkers, I argue that "farmworker-to-table," or sustainably *and* ethically provisioned Mexican-inspired cuisine, has the transformational potential to protect not just the land but also the people who work on it. The Mexican dining experiences at my study's conclusion demonstrate how the coloniality of power can be reconfigured and reimagined in our foodways so that new visions of hemispheric inclusion may emerge.

Chapter 2, "On Cinco de Drinko and Jimmiechangas: Culinary Brownface in the Rust Belt Midwest," argues that Mexican restaurants catering to non-Mexican consumers constitute a style of cuisine that I refer to here as "culinary brownface." My definition of culinary brownface converses with William Nericcio's critique of the United States' propaganda campaign against Latinx and Mexicans as exposed in his study *Tex[t]-Mex: Seductive Hallucinations of the "Mexican" in America* (2007). His chapter "Autopsy of a Rat: Sundry Parables of Warner Brothers Studios, Jewish American Animators, Speedy Gonzales, Freddy Lopez, and Other Chicano/Latino Marionettes Prancing about Our First World Visual Emporium; Parable Cameos by Jacques Derrida; and, a Dirty Joke" interrogates the vaudeville-esque patterns of dehumanization and commodification employed by midcentury Hollywood's exploitation of ethnic stereotypes. Both Terre Haute, Indiana, and Lima, Ohio, so-called "rust belt" towns, have experienced declining industry since the mid-twentieth century due to a variety of factors, such as the transfer of manufacturing to other parts of the United States, increased automation, the decline of the U.S. steel and coal industries, neoliberal policies such as NAFTA, and outsourcing. Meanwhile, these regions have witnessed a growth in Mexican residents, with an estimated 10 percent of the United States' Mexican population now living in the Midwest. Heritage food practices play a stabilizing role in the adjustment process of peoples experiencing the consequences of geographic and social displacement, even as migrants frequently own, staff, and perform ersatz ethnicity in brownface establishments. Drawing on field work, food journalism, interviews with restaurant workers, and literatures on the commodification of Mexicanness in popular culture, my chapter demonstrates that Anglo midwestern patronage of culinary brownface establishments conveys desires for Mexican food products that are styled and presented in ways that accommodate capitalist fantasies and maintain Anglo hegemony.

Chapter 3, "Homegirl Café: La Conciencia Mestiza as Culinary Counterstory," argues that Homegirl Café reinvents and reinvests in "homegirl" symbolism to create a new Angelino identity that associates working-class Latinas with liberatory food practices as a path to economic independence and cultural dignity. Whereas the "chola/o" figure is typically identified with racial tension and negative profiling in the public sphere, Homeboy Industries reinvests in youths of color, not as dangerous people to be feared but as community builders with educational and career prospects. By associating homegirls with sustenance, gainful employment, and alternatives to incarceration, Homegirl Café "flips the script" that has historically coidentified working-class Latinas with gang activity, detention, and dependency. To do this, my chapter interrogates mainstream appropriations of Latinas via the tropes of erotic tropicalism in the form of Chiquita bananas and the mandates of self-abnegation and domesticity implied in Nestlé's Abuelita chocolate. Unlike these dominant visual representations of Latina imagery in the culinary marketplace, the homegirl signifier generates a Chicana feminist social identity that recuperates formerly excluded complexities and celebrates homegirl defiance in the public sphere.

Chapter 4, "From Juan Valdez to Third Wave Cafés: Lattes and Latinidad in the Marketplace," analyzes the history of first, second, and third wave coffee advertisements that rely on the images of Latin Americans to make guarantees to consumers about the trade practices, freshness, and fairness of product lines. Beginning with the 1959 creation of Juan Valdez, a fictitious coffee grower created by the National Federation of Coffee Growers of Colombia for advertising in the United States, the long-running series of television ads depicting the iconic farmer with his serape, moustache, and mule named Conchita set the tone for how Latinos are deployed to stimulate coffee consumption in the United States. The first wave of coffee peaked in North America when freeze-dried coffee became the stock beverage across U.S. households after World War II. Advertisements featured ecstatic housewives enjoying the luxury of "good to the last drop" instant coffee, and diners and doughnut shops were the destinations for public coffee consumption. Thanks to the vision of the Doyle Dane Bernbach ad agency, the Valdez advertisements featured their protagonist sharing details about his coffee harvest, such as the ways in which soil, bean varietals, and altitude make a critical difference in the beverage's taste. Starbucks and Peets followed in this vision as Valdez's second wave drew attention to the benefits of specific types of beans and harvesting methods. Now, third wave coffee vendors focus on special-origin beans, roasting styles, importation, and detailed narratives about the company's relations with growers in the developing world. To do this convincingly, images of Guatemalan, Colombian, and unnamed indigenous and mestizo coffee workers and growers serve to bolster consumer confidence in labels such as "shade grown," "fair trade," and "direct trade," even while many of the corporate coffee companies are, in fact, competing with or undermining the benefits and reach of fair trade. Moreover, the café dining room images of humble-but-happy workers follow in the tradition of racial Others in food advertising (such as Aunt Jemima and the Chiquita Banana) that fulfill the noblesse oblige fantasy of consumers in the Global North to "own" mestizo bodies from a safe distance while imagining that their coffee consumption is a charitable endeavor.

In concert, my chapters examine diverse representations of the mestizo subject in contemporary systems of food production and preparation in order to identify some of the hidden and overt colonial orderings in our food chains. It's a fight to invigorate both imagination and action around the most utopian, yet most fundamental, of human rights: a world in which everyone is fed, and no one is harmed. Consider yourself tagged in.

FARMWORKER-TO-TABLE MEXICAN

Decolonizing Haute Cuisine

On Campesinos, Locavores, and the Staying Power of the Plantation System

Mexican and Chicana/o citizens and denizens of the United States get a sad laugh from the national condition that embraces its love affair with Mexican food at the same time as it evinces obsessive hostility toward the presence of its people. In 2013 the Taco Bell fast-food chain was ranked sixth in the nation in terms of system-wide sales, beating out Dunkin' Donuts, KFC, Pizza Hut, and Chick-fil-A, with Chipotle occupying the sixteenth rank. Thirty-seventh and thirty-eighth positions were held by Del Taco and Qdoba Mexican Grill, respectively, with El Pollo Loco hanging on to the forty-first spot.[1] Family-owned taquerías dot the nation's boulevards, strip malls, highways, and byways, and fine dining, once reserved for European fare, is now seeing interpretations of Mexican "regional," "authentic," and/or "modern" cooking on menus geared toward the gastronomically chic. Place this data alongside the "Build a Wall" ethos of the Trump regime, which follows on the heels of the "Deporter-in-Chief" reputation earned by Obama's administration,[2] and you have an understanding of the continuum of enthusiasm and disdain that characterizes national regard for its Mexican contributions.

Since early childhood, I was always impressed by the palpable sensation that Mexican cooking had the power to afford a safety zone, a sensory dimension in which the presence of Mexican cultural patrimony meets with qualified tolerance. Mexican restaurants seemed as

An earlier version of this chapter was published as "Farmworker-to-Table Mexican: Decolonizing Haute Cuisine," in *The Routledge Companion to Latina/o Popular Culture*, ed. Frederick Aldama (New York: Routledge, 2016).

satellite consulates, where the main event was the food, but a residual side effect was the small window of permission open to other areas of expression such as language, music, fashion, visual art, and the geophysical presence of mestizo bodies both at work and leisure with family and friends. The cross-cultural and unembarrassed excitement for Mexican culinary achievements represented a situational moratorium on animosity toward mestizo and indigenous people, where the fantasy of homogeneity was lifted as all the gathered tribes reveled in the sensual spell of salsa and cilantro. But the irony was a sad one. If only bordered bodies could circulate as freely and exaltedly as burritos! If only our children were as beloved as our chalupas!

If food provides the safest way to "do" Mexicanness in the national context, it also presents ready clichés and stereotypes. In the mainstream imaginary, tequila and "chimichangas" are sure to evoke insinuations of serious hangovers and digestive distress. Racial slurs targeting Mexicans link the people to the beans. What do you call a group of stoned Mexicans? Baked beans. What do you call a Mexican baptism? Bean dip. Why do Mexicans re-fry their beans? Have you seen a Mexican do anything right the first time? The Mexican food imaginary is not consistently respectful; its invocation is no guarantee of diversity, dignity, or pride.

This chapter connecting mestizo farm labor to Mexican fare acknowledges that the food we need to sustain life in the United States is the result of the arduous work performed by countless campesinos (peasant farmers). According to the United States Department of Agriculture Economic Research Service, farmworkers, consisting of field crop workers, nursery workers, livestock workers, farmworker supervisors, and hired farm managers, continue to be one of the most economically vulnerable population in the United States, with an hourly average earning for a nonsupervisory job reported at about $12.47 in 2017. The USDA reports that 49.2 percent of farmworkers and supervisors are U.S. citizens, with Hispanics constituting 63.8 percent of this workforce. Making up 15 percent of the entire U.S. population of wage and salary workers in 2016, we can see that the agricultural sector depends significantly on the work performed by peoples of Latin American origin.[3]

The objects of my research—restaurant establishments—mark a departure from the field of Latinx food studies that are typically inclined to focus on agri-food business practices, dietary choices, and marketing campaigns. Perhaps the scholarly reluctance has to do with the ready association of dining and consumption with the negative aspects of capitalist consumerism. Consumption, in the vein of critiques leveled at mainstream alternative food networks, evokes elite privilege, gourmandizing, and the feckless notion that fine dining can successfully substitute for more holistic challenges to conventional food provisioning. Haute cuisine, after all, denotes a social hierarchy established and preserved through access to elaborate preparations and presentations of the finest ingredients—the opposite of "low" gastronomic experiences.[4]

First, I review representative writings on Mexican foodways to historicize the location of the mestizo subject in relation to the production of food. Next, I argue that "farmworker-to-table," or sustainably and ethically provisioned Mexican-inspired cuisine, demonstrates that, while Enrique Olvera's historical 2015 opening of Cosme on Twenty-First Street may have been hailed by the *New Yorker* as "the undisputed opening of the season,"[5] Mexican food in the United States (and even in Mexico) continues to be regarded as a thoroughly vernacular cuisine, identified with hemispheric indigeneity and the hierarchies that Mexicanness in the United States evokes.

In conversation with Chicana mestizaje, the categories of gender and class inform my definition of decolonial practices that erode the logics of colonial and capitalist domination, as well as the privileges assigned to maleness. As noted in my introduction, the theoretical works of Walter Mignolo and Aníbal Quijano inform my definition of decolonial practices as those which interrogate or erode the project of Western capitalism in favor of communal access to resources, and supplant the monopoly of aesthetic priorities that secure Euro- and U.S.-centric management of the senses in favor of the inclusion of non-Western traditions and innovations.[6] If the politics of food production naturalize the invisibility of farm labor, they also do this with kitchen labor, where the epistemologies of food provisioning are often preserved and transmitted by women. Extremely valuable contributions are made by several women chefs discussed throughout this study who represent the forefront of decolonial culinary innovations, while "star chef" status in the preparation of Mexican food continues to be relegated almost exclusively to Anglos or Mexican men. The gender disparities in the culinary world are evident when we compare male and female average annual salaries of chefs and head cooks. In 2015 the average male salary was reported to be $32,707, while the female salary was only $26,078.[7] Moreover, of the 41,250 sexual harassment claims filed in the United States between 2005 and 2015, more than 14 percent came from the food service and hospitality sector—more than any other industry—and reports indicate that 40 percent of women experienced unwanted sexual behaviors in restaurant and hospitality jobs, with African American and Latina women more likely to be victims of unwanted sexual advances than White women.[8]

My "Mexican" food descriptor, at first blush, seems to be a straightforward designation, but a closer look reveals a term that is heavily contested. Gustavo Arellano emphasizes adaptation, interpreting Mexican-branded foods like Taco Bell and Chi-Chi's as a continuum of cultural exchange or, as Michael Soldatenko writes, "no less legitimate than its sibling in Mexico."[9] Food writing in feminist Chicana memoirs frequently frames culinary knowledge as a woman-centered connection to matrilineal memory, where the kitchen is reworked as a space of agency and even resistance to patriarchal values.[10] Jeffrey Pilcher defines Mexican culinary practices as the result of the encounter between Spanish and indigenous Mexican palates, cultures, and classes,[11] while Chicano poet José Antonio Burciaga's "After Aztlán" (1992) demonstrates the author's tendency to deploy traditional foods to establish a Chicano point of view:

> After Aztlán
> there will be no Mictlán,
> just the question
> at the last judgment
> about how you want
> your frijoles: con
> red chile, green chile,
> tortillas de harina, maiz, o pan?[12]

Meanwhile, Chicano poet Paul Martinez Pompa challenges the Chicano-as-tortilla-eater convention as well as the motif of matronly food preparation in "The Abuelita Poem" (2009). The following excerpt comes from the first section of the poem titled "Skin & Corn," which inserts tongue-in-cheek magical realism to describe how the abuelita kneads the masa:

> Her brown skin glistens as the sun
> pours through the kitchen window
> like gold leche. After grinding
> the _nixtamal_, a word so beautifully ethnic
> it must not only be italicized but underlined
> to let you, the reader, know you've encountered
> something beautifully ethnic, she kneads
> with the hands of centuries-old ancestor
> spirits who magically yet realistically possess her
> until the masa is smooth as a lowrider's
> chrome bumper. And I know she must do this
> with care because it says so on a website
> that explains how to make homemade corn tortillas.[13]

If tortillas enjoy the power to foster cultural cohesion, they are also just as capable of exposing tired cultural clichés. Martinez Pompa expresses exhaustion with the motif of the abuelita and her cooking as the embodied archive of traditional knowledge. Here, the abuelita of his poem learns her tortilla recipe on a website, where she also learns that she is supposed to imbue the ritual act of their preparation with maternal and ancestral affection and gravitas.

In spite of these divergent attitudes toward "Mexican food," two major themes among observers appear with consistency. The first is the reality that Mexican cuisine within the United States, whether in traditionalist, experimental, or massified dimensions, is marked by conditions of coloniality, with the "Mexican" designation signifying both Spanish and indigenous clashes as well as the vertical orderings of U.S. capital. Another consistent theme surfacing across Mexican foodscapes is the centrality of maize (corn) to Mexican and Chicana/o cultural identity. This is certainly the claim of Roberto Cintli Rodriguez's _Our Sacred Maíz Is Our Mother: Indigeneity and Belonging in the Americas_ (2014), where the author maintains that, more than a sum of numerous wars of invasion, it was the seven-thousand-year-old maize culture that connects Mexican peoples to their hemispheric indigeneity and represents the core expression of cultural knowledge and cohesion.

The history of maize is also the history of the Mesoamerican civilizing project. Domesticated in central Mexico by around 6500 BCE, successful maize, beans, squash, and chili crops prompted the sedentary organization of village life. By 1500 BCE the Olmec were contributing monumental architecture and the Mesoamerica's first state-organized society, which would not have been possible without maize surpluses.[14] The nixtamalization process involves cooking maize in an alkaline solution, thereby increasing its content of assimilable protein and its malleability. After grinding it on a metate (grinding stone), the maize dough was formed into tortillas, tamales, and other variations that spread through much of North America in the first millennium CE.[15] Elizabeth Fitting's "Cultures of Corn and Anti-GMO Activism in Mexico and Columbia" (2014) argues that the ongoing transnational campaign against Monsanto, Dow Chemical, and DuPont's commercial transgenic (GMO) maize crops constitutes a defense of the country's preeminent symbol of place. Viewing traditional varieties of corn as a symbol of national sovereignty, activist slogans such as "We are people of corn," and "Without corn there is no country," attest to the continuity of maize not only as a biological resource but also as the foundation of regional Mesoamerican identity and autonomy.[16] As Zilkia Janer summarizes in her volume *Latino Food Culture*, "Maize is the staple that gives Latino cuisine a cohesive identity."[17] While this may be true for a pan-Latina/o assessment of hemispheric foodways, it is especially the case for Mexican society and culture, where maize was first domesticated.

While Mexican food in the United States has a history that is far-reaching, transnational, and as fluid as the peoples that experience its bordered realities, two distinct lines of development characterize the major Mexican dining approaches. For some, eating habits remain much as they would in the various regions of Mexico, reflecting steady migratory patterns of Mexican nationals and their dietary patterns. The other consumption style is one that has adapted to Anglo culinary norms and cultural and/or geographic distancing from traditional Mexican ingredients.[18] These two tendencies need not be mutually exclusive. It is not an anomaly for a household to enjoy traditional chilaquiles made of fried corn tortilla pieces in simmering salsa on one day and a "breakfast burrito" of egg and chorizo wrapped in a large flour tortilla from a drive-through window on the next. Across

U.S. Mexican diets, some ingredients and practices that continue to be popular in Mexico are seldom found in the U.S. urban context, such as gathering eggs from the family coop, using freshly slaughtered poultry, and preparing food in outdoor pits. Also, following prevailing dietary recommendations, the use of lard is less extensive across Mexican American contemporary cooking than in Mexican national cuisine.[19] Ilan Stavans offers the observation that "a Mexican will remind you that a burrito isn't really a wrap but a small donkey and that a margarita is a flower not a drink."[20] In each of the iterations of Mexican cuisine in the United States, accommodations and adaptations are made by both household and restaurant cooks to reflect the geographically specific pleasures and priorities of the people they feed.

As a modifier of Mexican food, "farm-to-table" does not constitute a particular preparation or aesthetic tendency but rather refers to the campaign across farms, restaurants, grocery stores, and other institutions to reduce waste and demand values-based guarantees at all stages of food production, including harvesting, storage, processing, packaging, transportation, marketing, sales, and consumption. The expression emphasizes the need for freshness, which entails the swift handling of vegetables and fruits, and the notion that crisp, live flavors are best when they are newly harvested. Another implication is ecological. By transitioning from industrialized and globalized provisioning to the localized foodshed, "locavores" claim that the environment benefits when food is not shipped over long distances, reasoning that the carbon "foot" treads lighter without the use of harmful preservatives and the combustion of noxious fuels to bring food to the dining room. In contemporary food journalism, farm-to-table is also employed to refer to restaurants that emphasize seasonality and more direct presentations of food that eschew "food-as-art" displays characteristic of rarefied atmospheres of gastronomic prestige. At other times, farm-to-table is merely shorthand for a reasonable commitment to fresh and/or quality ingredients and a stylish environment.

Industry trends reveal enormous consumer conviction in farm-to-table provisioning, as confirmed by the National Restaurant Association's 2013 report, which demonstrates that both consumers and the American Culinary Federation chefs are demanding more local sourcing and sustainable farming practices in their food products than ever before.[21] But the farm-to-table ethos is not without its opponents. The mainstream farm-to-table disparagers exhibit anxieties about what is optimal for the human body and what is helpful to the earth, yet seldom challenge worker exploitation that thrives at the heart of our food chains. Dan Barber, author of the acclaimed *The Third Plate: Field Notes on the Future of Food* (2014), writes in the *New York Times* that "farm-to-table advocates are often guilty of ignoring a whole class of humbler crops that are required to produce the most delicious food," and recommends the cultivation of cowpeas, millet, and mustard in order to solve farm-to-table's shortcomings.[22] Hannah Palmer Egan, food blogger for New York City's *Village Voice*, laments that the farm-to-table tagline is mistreated when used to describe a perfunctory inclusion of a few locally sourced items rather than a real commitment:

> Still, there's a difference between adding a few token Greenmarket ingredients to the menu and pushing the envelope when it comes to local sourcing, and some restaurants are working faster and going further to get produce from area farmers and give diners the freshest possible experience.[23]

In spite of the conditions of farmworkers who remain, according to the U.S. Department of Agriculture, "among the most economically disadvantaged working groups in the United States," complaints about farm-to-table tend to focus on problems of soil erosion or failures in freshness and totally ignore how the ethics of eating impact the life chances of agricultural laborers.[24]

Insisting that social responsibility also be included at the local food-laden table, Devon Peña, Daniel Faber, David Goodman, E. Melanie DuPuis, and Michael Goodman figure among those changing the conversation in order to address the problem of working conditions on farms, restaurants, and related food delivery environments. Evaluating theoretical trajectories in the area of food studies in the United States and the United Kingdom, Goodman, DuPuis, and Goodman charge that too many Alternative Food Networks (AFNs) are narrowly focused on affixing boutique labels, certificates, and quality assurances to high-price-point dining experiences rather than transforming the logic of domination in food production to something that is qualitatively different. In other words, the farm-to-table designation figures among the AFNs most associated with premium foods at prohibitive prices: the updated and earth-conscious construal of "gourmet."

While contemporary AFNs have played a significant role in raising awareness about the dangers of conventional production values, the tenor of their campaigns remains rooted in the neoliberal logic of coloniality: majoritarian AFNs remain discursively rooted in natural resource conservation, wilderness preservation, and professional environmentalism, with food provisioning attitudes contingent on elite dietary preferences and consumer, rather than worker, safety.[25] A representative example comes from the documentary *The New Green Giants: Is Organic Better?* (directed by Ted Remerowski, 2015), in which the Environmental Working Group (known as the Dirty Dozen) touts the importance of reducing exposure to pesticides, even after a Stanford research paper has concluded that there are no nutritional benefits to consuming organic food over conventional.[26] The numerous resultant headlines declaring that organic foods are not worth the higher prices paid for them belies the reality that farmworkers who mix, load, or apply pesticides suffer more chemical-related injuries, illnesses, and deaths than any other workforce in the nation. Daniel Faber reported in 1998 that more than three hundred thousand of this population suffer from pesticide poisoning each year, and between eight hundred and one thousand incidents of pesticide poisoning are fatal.[27] Furthermore, the scope of workers injured each year by pesticides is difficult to track, because no national surveillance system takes into account reports of suspected pesticide poisoning along with factors such as lack of health insurance, language barriers, and fear of job loss or deportation that impact workers' ability and willingness to seek medical care.[28] Mainstream AFNS such as the Dirty Dozen prioritize what consumers eat and the toll of pesticides on the environment, but offer a limited critique about the human toll of conventional agribusiness on its most vulnerable workers.

This is Devon G. Peña's critique of mainstream environmentalism and AFNs in *Mexican Americans and the Environment: Tierra y Vida* (2005). He credits Rachel Carson's pioneering *Silent Spring* (1962) with providing a bold and pivotal study that established a link between "economic poisons" (pesticides) and health problems such as cancer and reproductive system disorders that cause birth defects, but points out that Carson limits the conversation to the consequences borne by women and juvenile consumers, and, as with the Dirty Dozen's efforts, does not acknowledge the mestizo-dominant agricultural workforce that suffers the most frequent and serious consequences from overexposure to chemical toxins.[29]

The ability to not "see" farm labor and the struggles of those who perform it is pandemic. While traveling a blistering expanse of California's U.S. Route 101 north of the Oxnard Plain, I was able to observe many farmworkers performing agricultural labor, their bodies bent under the sun's punishing rays. My destination was a home where my friend was a hired house sitter for a Santa Barbara family. There, a particular book title on the house's shelf caught my attention. It was Zachiah Murray's *Mindfulness in the Garden: Zen Tools for Digging in the Dirt* (2012). With an introduction by Thich Nhat Hanh, the volume offers "simple mindfulness verses (gathas) composed to connect the mind and body and to bring the reader/gardener's awareness to the details of the present moment as they work in the garden." The activities of softening and preparing the ground and watering the seeds bring the reader to a close communion with nature and "ultimately to one's self through the love and understanding they evoke."[30] Here, agricultural endeavors are idealized to the extent that they are on par with a yoga class or a meditation retreat. The earth, garden, and natural world are evoked as ways to be in communion with the "self," and the self is the ultimate destination of the reader's journey through the dirt. In the scorching heat and enduring drought, it was difficult to imagine more punishing employment than the work farm laborers undertook alongside the 101. A publication extolling the virtues of gardening as a meditative pastime juxtaposed with the abjectness of agricultural laborers bespeaks the disconnect between elite society, its Edenic ideas about gardening and seasonality, and the realities of agricultural employment. Murray's readership is coded as White and privileged: agricultural employment is exotic, unpaid, recreational, and leads to the aggrandizement of the self. The other group—the one characterized by subsistence pay, rampant occupational hazards, and the invisibility of the self—is not the constituency Murray is interested in leading toward a more heightened state of consciousness about cultivation.

In the Western mainstream "alternative" narrative, the "self" is the ultimate accomplishment, and the natural world is a route toward this purpose. Investigating health inequalities and the U.S.-Mexico border, medical anthropologist Seth Holmes exposes the physical deterioration that is an inevitable consequence of performing farm labor.

> After the first week of picking on the farm, I asked two young female pickers how their knees and backs felt. One replied that she could no longer feel anything ("Mi cuerpo ya no puede sentir nada"), though her knees still hurt sometimes. The other said that her knees, back, and hips are always hurting ("Siempre me duelen"). Later that same afternoon, one of the young Triqui men I saw playing basketball every day the week before the harvest told me that he and his friends could no longer run because their bodies hurt so much ("Ya no corremos; no aguantamos"). In fact, even the vistas that were so sublime and beautiful to me had come to mean ugliness, pain, and work to the pickers. On multiple occasions, my Triqui companions responded with confusion to my exclamations about the area's beauty and explained that the fields were "pure work" (puro trabajo).[31]

For farmworkers the ugliness and pain of their working lives erode the spiritual connectivity and dignity that elite and recreational conservationists insist is their right to enjoy. And if severe conditions produce despair among workers who have migrated out of economic necessity, there are many who have been forced to perform labor under circumstances that can only be described as modern-day slavery.

In 1993 tomato crop workers in Florida organized to form the Coalition of Immokalee Workers (CIW) in order to demand social responsibility among growers and corporations, a stop to human trafficking, and protections against gender-based violence in the fields. In 2007 they were presented with the Anti-Slavery Award by Anti-Slavery International for their work uncovering and bringing to justice six separate modern slavery operations under which four hundred farmworkers were held in captivity in Florida and South Carolina and forced to pick vegetables and citrus for ten to twelve hour days under armed surveillance. Their pay was an approximate twenty dollars a week; attempts at escape were met with violent repression.[32]

The Florida Immokolee workers should be read not as an anomaly but rather as the continuity of historical labor practices that characterize national economic activity rooted in the earliest days of large-scale agricultural operations that denied enslaved peoples a pathway to citizenship status, enfranchisement, or the hope of escape from the plantation system. In the wake of federal antislavery laws, migrant farm laborers, largely of Latin American descent, fill the positions that had once depended on enslaved labor. The Depression years witnessed the mass deportations and the "repatriation" of more than eighty-nine thousand Mexicans, but when the United States needed to prepare for war overseas, it came knocking on the U.S.-Mexico border again to solicit workers for the agricultural, manufacturing, and service industries.[33] The Bracero Program (1942–64) supplied the United States with temporary contract laborers,[34] while its companion project Operation Wetback (1954) sought to aggressively detain and deport undocumented workers.[35]

The two-pronged threat of pesticide poisoning and the vulnerabilities of undocumented status are at the heart of the historical Chicano challenge to mainstream AFNs. Of approximately 2 million farmworkers in the United States, 90 percent are people of color, and the majority live under the severe restrictions of an undocumented legal status. Laura Pulido (1996) notes that in the 1960s, Cesar Chavez's United Farm Workers Organizing Committee (UFWOC) focused on pesticides both as a demand and a tool for struggle. Lawsuits and administrative actions, boycotts, contract negotiations, sit-ins, picketing, and fasts figured among the strategies employed by the UFWOC in their struggle to gain safer working conditions and adequate pay. While the union's legacy is one of mixed results, their activities helped curtail chemically intensive farming systems, shift California pesticide regulation away from its close alignment with growers and chemical companies, and compel the University of California to commit to sustainable cultivation in their research pursuits because of the severe health risks imposed on workers.

In light of colonial orderings that place mestizo and indigenous bodies in the highest zones of health and safety risk, scholarship on food provisioning demonstrates that a growing number of researchers interpret food not only as sustenance but also as a means to counter the negative effects of industrialized consumption and cultural abjection. Incisive historical investigations are offered by Jeffrey Pilcher, Jaime Vilchis, Rafael Chabrán, Elizabeth Coonrod Martínez, and Gustavo Arellano, while Meredith E. Abarca applies a framework of radical feminist epistemology to interpret women's transmission of hemispheric foodways. Encarnación Pinedo, Zilkia Janer, Laura Esquivel, and Stephanie M. Sánchez figure among writers who interpret Mexican identity through the lens of culinary craft. Conducting nutritional research, Frederick Trowbride, Fernando Mendoza, Julie Collins-Dogrul, and Kenia Saldaña demonstrate that obesity rates and susceptibility to other diseases increase as Mexican American families adopt more mainstream, U.S. food choices. Offering an Américas-based critique of the coloniality of mainstream foodways, Luz Calvo edits the *Decolonize Your Diet* website that applies critical race theory to the disease load that is the inevitable consequence of the Standard American Diet (the "SAD" diet). Calvo rediscovers and reclaims traditional Mexican and indigenous foods as a revolutionary endeavor; both her website and recipe book co-authored with Catriona Rueda Esquibel locate traditional foodways as a fundamental path to decolonization: "Indigenous and African traditions in spirituality, music, literature, and food were never completely suppressed by the colonizers but kept alive, sometimes surreptitiously, in daily acts of resistance that include storytelling, recipe sharing, and ceremony."[36] Vanessa Fonseca and Enrique C. Ochoa investigate the massification of food within the context of global capitalism and neocolonial priorities that disassociate Mexican-branded products from their Mesoamerican origins,[37] and Devon Peña examines the Chicano Environmental Justice Movement's linkage of environmental, economic, and social justice issues as a new alternative to mainstream environmentalism.[38]

As the farm-to-table designation evokes the scenario of elite diners eager to deepen consumer privilege, the farmworker-to-table expression serves to sound the sacrifices of a largely mestizo origin workforce in urgent need of awareness and advocacy, as conventional and even alternative provisioning models cleave to colonial blind spots. Farmworker-to-table, however, is not just a play on the AFN that currently enjoys market popularity. It is also a way to signal the identities of campesinos in hemispheric foodways as people who have long connected decolonial resistance to the plight of the land. The campesina and campesino came to epitomize the mestizo condition in early resistance movements, and many observers agree that the civil disobedience, hunger strikes, boycotts, picket lines, and other grassroots organizing measures deployed by César Chávez and Dolores Huerta to unionize farm laborers and advocate for migrant workers' rights signaled the beginning of the Chicano identity (Beltrán; Acuña; Ontiveros). Chicana artist Ester Hernandez grew up in a family of farmworkers, contributing to the protest aesthetic visible in her iconic screen print *Sun Mad* (1981). The poster depicts a skeleton in a sun bonnet who gleefully harvests grapes contaminated with pesticides. El Teatro Campesino ("Farmworkers' Theater") formed in 1965 to bring visibility to the needs of farmworkers during the five-year Delano grape strike and boycott in Central California. The poet Alurista's "El plan espiritual de Aztlán" provides a foundational narrative of Chicano nationalism, in which it is declared, "We are free and sovereign to determine those tasks which are justly called for by our house, our land, the sweat of our brows, and by our hearts. Aztlán belongs to those who plant the seeds, water the fields, and gather the crops and not foreign Europeans."[39] In short, campesino advocacy among Chicano rights advocacy exemplifies Emiliano Zapata's creed: the land belongs to those who work on it, and the United Farmworkers (UFW) symbol has the potency to champion not only the struggle for farmworkers' rights but also the struggle for the dignity and determination of all Chicano and mestizo peoples.

Decolonizing Haute Cuisine

According to Alan Warde, food consumption provides the ultimate metaphor for the concept of taste.[40] If this is the case, then in culinary establishments celebrated for excellence, chefs are auteurs of multisensory atmospheres who play a vital role in influencing what a generation craves. My interpretation of colonial ideology in Mexican fine dining is examined here in the context of restaurant websites, Internet review services, industry journalism, and personal interviews. These sources delineate a border zone that freely touts Anglo-origin cooks as redeemers of Mexican authentic cuisine while evincing skepticism about Mexican-origin cooks in the high-level culinary world.

As a way of knowing and a route for the communication of cultural coherence, discourses surrounding Mexican cuisine with Anglo chefs describe that which is "discovered" or "found," much in the way the Americas are cast in terms of the discovery of people and wildlife, rather than the culmination of knowledges that have been honed over the course of millennia. In contrast, when press, public, and critics turn toward Mexican-origin chefs, their restaurants and menus are read against the prevailing mainstream understandings of the Mexican diet that, in the United States, seldom demonstrates fidelity to historic Mesoamerican foodways. And while the millennial aughts and early teens have seen the emergence of new Mexican and Chicana/o actors in the culinary landscape, Anglo chefs continue to dominate upscale offerings. Gustavo Arellano notes that "the Mexican cookbook industry, a multimillion-dollar operation whose bookshelves expand every year, is an overwhelmingly American-written one."[41] Spanish-surnamed cooks continue to be in the minority in the publication of Mexican cookbooks and as proprietors of establishments associated with culinary expertise. Even in New Mexico, a state that takes great pride in its slogan of "red or green," a survey of the twenty-six restaurants participating in Santa Fe's Farm to Restaurant program reveals that only three businesses specialized in fine Mexican cuisine, and all of these had non-Mexican chefs at the helm.[42]

Among non-Mexican chefs and restaurant proprietors, it is routine for their promotional materials to provide their "found Mexican" story. This is where Anglo cooks narrate a traveler's tale about their interactions with Mexican cooking and carefully construct a "romantic crusader" image of the intrepid entrepreneur. Positional superiority is naturalized via the discourse of discovery. The most famous example is Rick Bayless, who is credited as the first to bring Mexican cuisine into the realm of fine dining in the United States. Bayless, owner of Frontera Grill and Topolobampo in Chicago, also sells the Frontera food product line offering marinades, salsas, tortilla chips, and other specialties bearing his brand that enjoys distribution by major supermarket chains such as Walmart, Publix, Target, and Safeway. His website states, "Most people know Rick Bayless from winning the title of Bravo's *Top Chef Masters*, beating out the French and Italian with his authentic Mexican cuisine."[43] An Internet visitor is to understand that although French and Italian cuisines are the reigning titleholders, it is a credit to Bayless's talent that he manages to achieve this title with vernacular Mexican food. His discovery of Mexican cuisine is touted by journalist Craig Claiborne in the *New York Times* as "the greatest contribution to the Mexican table imaginable."[44] Raised in an Oklahoma restaurant family, Bayless studied Spanish and Latin American studies as an undergraduate before pursuing a doctoral degree in Anthropological Linguistics at the University of Michigan. With his wife Deann, he lived in Mexico for six years, where they researched the recipes that would turn into his first cookbook, *Authentic Mexican: Regional Cooking from the Heart of Mexico* (1987). The website celebrates the Baylesses' discovery of Mexican food, which is attributed to their "extended stay in Mexico," but neglects to provide remark about the teachers who generously shared their foodways with the researchers.

> It was 1987. Rick Bayless and his wife, Deann Groen Bayless, had just returned from an extended stay in Mexico, where they had been researching their first book. They wanted a restaurant that tasted and felt like their travels. So they hung colorful Mexican folk art on the walls, turned up the Mariachi music and packed the menu with the foods that reminded them of their travels: tangy tomatillos, rich black beans, fiery chiles.[45]

Bayless is routinely credited with establishing one of the first upscale Mexican restaurants in the country. He opened Frontera Grill in 1987 with retrieved "folk art" and "Mariachi music" and Topolobampo in 1989 as its "sleek, classy sister." As of 2015 Topolobampo has one Michelin star—a high achievement in a culinary ranking system that has performed inspections since 1900. That non-Mexicans can prepare Mexican food with expertise is not, in and of itself, an imposition of superiority. Instead, it is the stream of Bayless's lionizing claims to authenticity based on his discovery that bears the imprint of coloniality.

This "crossing over" of Mexican cooking into the higher echelons of culinary sophistication is a familiar phenomenon to observers of the "Latin music boom," wherein performers such as Susana Baca, Selena Quintana, and Marc Anthony, who had enjoyed great success and relevance in Latin American contexts, were repackaged as "debut artists" and "discoveries" upon signing with major English-language U.S. labels or appearing on pop (as opposed to "Latin") music charts.[46] This "Columbus effect" grants the importance of "discovery" to those of European descent: "Once discovered by Europeans, the Other finally enters the human world."[47]

For Linda Tuhiwai Smith, the claims by Western researchers to authority in the cultural production of indigenous communities represent the continuation of colonial expansionism.[48] The Western observer frequently sees the benefits of their contribution as representing an emancipatory ideal, as somehow "saving" a newly "discovered" and oppressed community. This narrative is observable in the work of Bayless, who is styled as the "rescuer" of mestizo foodways from their massification and corruption, and thereby acts as a savior, rather than an oppressor, of native knowledge. Tuhiwai Smith writes:

> It galls us that Western researchers and intellectuals can assume to know all that is possible to know of us, on the basis of their brief encounters with some of us. It appalls us that the West can desire, extract and claim ownership of our ways of knowing, our imagery, the things we create and produce, and then simultaneously reject the people who created and developed those ideas and seek to deny them further opportunities to be creators of their own culture and own nations.[49]

Bayless's recourse to indigenous knowledge is told from the perspective of a knower—as an arbiter of what is regional, authentic, and worthy of transcending blue collar associations with Mexican cuisine in the United States. Following the pattern of extraction and ownership described by Tuhiwai Smith, native knowers are unnamed and unsung, and native ways of knowing are reproduced by the colonial researcher while the people who developed these foodways are simultaneously rejected.

Likewise, Mary Sue Milliken and Susan Feniger are co-chefs and co-owners of the critically acclaimed and wildly popular Border Grill restaurants, who "found" Mexican cuisine as though it had been lying dormant without a custodian, waiting for them to arrive and rescue it from neglect. With resort dining establishments serving "modern Mexican food" in Las Vegas, downtown Los Angeles, and Santa Monica, California, their website materials announce that "Mary Sue and Susan are preeminent ambassadors of Mexican cuisine, setting the standard for gourmet Mexican fare for over two decades and authoring five cookbooks, including *Cooking with Too Hot Tamales* and *Mesa Mexicana*."[50] As Anglo captains of Mexican fine dining, they are ascribed with skill, artistry, and brilliance.

> Ironically, it was in French restaurants where Chefs Mary Sue Milliken and Susan Feniger first tasted authentic Latin flavors. While guests were dining on escargot out front, in the back of the house Mary Sue and Susan were discovering the home cooking of Oaxaca and the Yucatan at staff meals prepared by their fellow cooks from Mexico. . . . In 1985, Mary Sue and Susan packed a VW bug and took a road trip far south of the Mexican border. Never setting foot in a "fine restaurant," they learned the recipes and techniques of market vendors and home cooks, from street corners in downtown Mexico City to back road family barbecues and taco stands along the beach. When they returned, they opened Border Grill and "applied the same intelligence," noted *Los Angeles Magazine*, "to green corn tamales and cactus-paddle tacos that other chefs might to a lobe of foie gras."[51]

The "intelligence" here is not attributed to the Oaxacans and Yucatecans in the back of the house, but to the French-trained Milliken and Feniger for capitalizing on their traditions. Once again, Mexican knowledge is made to appear as though it pertained to the public domain.

When Mexican and Chicana chefs are at the helm, a different set of narratives prevail. The review of San Jose's upscale Zona Rosa restaurant conducted by Jennifer Graue sums up a mainstream notion about what Mexican dining should entail:

Americans tend to make assumptions about Mexican restaurants: that they are cheap and cheerful; that the food is fast and filling; and that the chips and salsa are free and free-flowing.[52]

Graue's appraisal begins with an acknowledgement of the stereotypes that, by 2013, continued to dominate popular interpretations of Mexican fare. "Cheap," "cheerful," and with a fast and complimentary appetizer, the "chips, margaritas, and guac" are expectations that diners cling to when it comes to Mexican fare, while Anglo chefs are not burdened with the responsibility of explaining that their food is not cheap.

Even the celebrity chef Enrique Olvera of Cosme, whose restaurant Pujol in Mexico City was ranked number twenty on the 2014 San Pellegrino World's 50 Best Restaurants list, is powerless to change this narrative. Like Graue, Ryan Sutton begins his review by visiting the stereotypes.

So Cosme is a new Mexican restaurant in an old strip club space. Are the margaritas and guac any good? We'll get to that later, but this isn't really that type of joint. . . . Dinner for two after tax and tip probably won't cost less than $200, making Cosme one of USA's most expensive Mexican spots. But this Flatiron hangout isn't more expensive than, say, Estela or any other ambitious small-plates establishment that doesn't happen to be Mexican.[53]

Sutton concludes his article with a remark about the guacamole at Cosme: it exists, but it is relegated to a less-than-prominent place on the menu, and the house staff conveys a lack of enthusiasm for this stock feature of less ambitious menus. The reviewer then warns the readers of the price point, anticipating a surprise reaction at the prospect of a Mexican dining experience being so dear.

Amelia Lester's review that appeared in the *New Yorker* does not begin with a riff on the clichés, but prepares the reader for the status diners that have turned out for Cosme's first season:

Should Cosme need a mascot, the man at the next table
will do, in his fedora and mock turtleneck, looking like an
angel investor on "Silicon Valley" and asking for another
round of premium tequila shots. If you build an expensive place in the Flatiron district, he will come.[54]

Lester goes on to quip that the conspicuous affluence on parade in
the dining room does not detract from Olvera's food: his smoked raw
sepia (cuttlefish) is described by the reviewer as "a tangle of translu-
cent, silvered strands, tossed with the simplest of tomato salsas. The
taste of the ocean announces itself as a zephyr, not a squall." Lester is
equally enthralled by the octopus cocktail with purple and blue corn
and charred avocado, and later the cornhusk meringue made with
mousse of mascarpone, cream, and a corn purée that "spills out like
lava from its core." The reviews are careful to explain that prices are
high and the atmosphere elite: not the warnings they need to issue
when discussing the latest in European fine dining experiences.

In sum, fine dining prepared by Anglo chefs is narrated as a mis-
sionary achievement, with obvious correlation to Tuhiwai Smith's
depiction of the foreign researcher who styles him or herself as
the emancipator of Mexican cuisine. On the other hand, Mexican-
origin chefs are inscribed with the imprint of the border crossing and
"crossing over": by moving into the realm of high-end cuisine, they
are seen as matter out of place. Apologies are in order if Mexican
or Chicana chefs have the audacity to provide dining experiences
that rival the slow pace and high price points found in European
establishments.

As Cosme is well-positioned to shift the paradigm of high-end
dining in the United States to include experimental Mexican approaches, the decolonial objective of breaking the monopoly of Western aesthetic priorities in order to include indigenous traditions and
innovations is soundly achieved. However, the communal access to
resources, or endeavors to raise consciousness about the colonial configuration of resources and alter the politics of foodways, does not figure prominently as a core value of Olvera or his restaurants. While the
aesthetic movement is a significant one, and indeed addresses the long
absence of Mexican culinary innovation from serious consideration
by accomplished reviewers, I argue that a decolonial haute cuisine

must also sustain a commitment to reconfiguring communities and challenge the logic of domination in the food chains.

More than an innovation of culinary fashion, decolonial Mexican cuisine must take part in a fight against the exploitation of land-based, hemispheric communities of color, and two women figure at the forefront of this movement. An extremely important contribution is made by Zarela Martinez, a top name in upscale Mexican dining since 1987 (the same year as Frontera Grill) when she opened her own restaurant on Manhattan's Upper East Side and served dishes such as fish with coconut and fresh mint and spicy pineapple salad that contrasted with the city's slate of ubiquitous snack foods such as tacos and burritos. A multiplatform celebrity chef, her thirteen-part PBS series, *Zarela! La Cocina Veracruzana*, takes viewers on walks through Veracruz, turning the camera on the markets, kitchens, and bakeries where traditional methods of cooking are maintained and celebrated by people whose recipes and techniques constitute a body of knowledge. By showing mestizo and indígena peoples as hemispheric, millennial stewards of a complex and sophisticated cuisine, Martinez acknowledges the cultural debts she owes for the success of her culinary art.

On the West Coast, the campesino-to-table commitment can be found at Dominica Rice-Cisneros's Cosecha Cafe. Located in downtown Oakland's Old Swan Market, Cosecha has steadily garnered deep affection and respect from community members, peers, and press since its opening in 2011. Featured in national and international travel guides such as the photo-driven guidebook *This Is Oakland: A Guide to the City's Most Interesting Places* (2014) and the *Wall Street Journal* (2012), mouthwatering descriptions of her sweet yam and Oaxaca cheese quesadillas made from handmade tortillas and zesty salsa verde, achiote-marinated chicken, blood orange and kumquat salad, and pumpkin seed and green chili mole bring a steady stream of diners who sit at wooden picnic tables or outside on the sidewalk along Fourth Street. Visitors order and pay at a counter while on the other side of a low glass partition, a Mexicana standing at the comal steadily turns out fresh tortillas by hand for each of the incoming orders. The atmosphere recalls the Mexican mercado (marketplace) eateries that Rice-Cisneros identifies as her inspiration. If Cosecha's high ceilings and semi-open-air dining mingling with the scent of mole verde and steaming tamales, contiguous to Oakland's historic resources, do not evoke the atmospherics of the Mexican mercado, the faded and pixelated printout of Mexico's patron saint la Virgen de Guadalupe unceremoniously affixed to the white tile behind the counter with Scotch tape is certain to seal the deal.

A graduate of San Francisco's California Culinary Academy, Rice-Cisneros interned at Eccolo in Berkeley, Stars in San Francisco, Daniel and Four Seasons in New York, and Soleil in Mexico City, but the training that receives the most attention is her internship at Alice Waters's Chez Panisse. The reigning first name in "farm-to-table," Waters is a founding author of the "California cuisine" style and the founder of the Edible Schoolyard Project and has had a pivotal role in shaping national consumer consciousness about the benefits of organic, local, whole foods.[55] Whereas Chez Panisse's pursuit to prepare items with the finest possible ingredients inspired relationships with the local and organic purveyors and growers at its inception in the 1970s, by the 1980s this aesthetically driven charge gave way to an insistence on Slow Food and the farm-restaurant connection as vehicles to save biodiversity and cultural conservation from the wreckage of "anonymous junk food" that was rapidly eroding environmental, cultural, and personal health.[56] This approach is evident in the relationships Rice-Cisneros has cultivated not only with farmers and purveyors but also with staff and community members.

> It's not just about making the food that will sell, it's about making what we want to eat. It's all Mexicanos doing the work, and later their family members are coming to visit and spend time here, and that influences what we feel like creating. There is a blend of the kitchen and the front, and we love to have that. Everyone comes together.[57]

Even with journalists and community members clearly touting Cosecha's offerings as Chez Panisse–quality fare (with the exception of Poonam G., who writes, "I came here on Cinco De Mayo, and it was very obvious they were not prepared for it. I would think that a Mexican restaurant would at least do some sort of preparation for it!"), the bulk of the negative responses to Cosecha on Yelp consistently have to do with prices. Susan D. claims that prices "are way out of line for counter service & communal seating," and complains about paying three dollars for chips, salsa, and guacamole. Allen C. laments that "prices here for tacos are much higher than at other places. Prices vary based on what kind of taco you get, but it's hard to convince me that $5 for a taco is ever a good deal. They get even more expensive at dinner too."

Cosecha's price point is a reflection of its dedication both to organic and ethical purveyors featured on their website and menus and fair wages for its employees. Rice-Cisneros tells a story of two of her Mexicana staff members being able to leave abusive relationships and support their families solely on the income that they receive at the restaurant with just as much pride as when she recounts how the lamb birria she made in the home of Waters was declared by her mentor to be "the best lamb I ever had." And the expectation that "cheap" must be the sacred priority of Mexican gastronomy is not limited to the swipes of Yelp reviewers criticizing Cosecha's audacity from a remote and anonymous electronic device—it also comes from Rice-Cisnero's fellow industry professionals in person. She recounts the experience of purchasing Cosecha ingredients from the San Francisco Bay Area's most reputable organic farms at Berkeley's Farmer's Market. Even though she runs into the same cadre of Anglo male chefs at the market every week, it is not uncommon for them to insist on a reaction of surprise and skepticism when they see her there, buying from the same high-end purveyors' stalls that they frequent.

In spite of skepticism about Mexican and Chicana/o chefs holding intellectual authority as high-end Mexican restaurateurs, Olvera, Martinez, and Rice-Cisneros represent only a few of the noteworthy figures exploring Mexican cuisine's cultural ideals and influencing public behaviors about Mesoamerican foodways. While Olvera's aesthetics realign colonial assumptions by championing indigenous foodways as a timely epistemic and aesthetic innovation, Martinez and Rice-Cisneros reconfigure gustatory prejudices at the same time as they promote communal knowledges and equitable distribution of resources. If, according to Meredith E. Abarca and Nieves Pascual Soler, food constitutes a "venue of communication" wherein knowledge is assimilated at the sensual level,[58] then the farmworker-to-table commitment constitutes a sensual venue of communication in which both the labors of farmworkers and the land on which they toil are safe from harm, and no Mexican gets discovered.[59]

ON CINCO DE DRINKO AND JIMMIECHANGAS

Culinary Brownface in the Rust Belt Midwest

Lima Losers, Meth Labs, and Culinary Brownface: A Tale of Two Cities

When I entered Terre Haute's Casita Taco (the sign had eroded so that it read "Casi Taco"), the pungent smell brought back memories of the public school cafeteria on chimichanga day. It took me by surprise that their signature item, according to the posted menu, was the "Wet Sancho." The item consisted of a seasoned ground beef wrapped in a flour tortilla and smothered in red sauce. As a person of Mexican descent familiar with Chicano slang, I was confused by the dish's appellation. "Sancho," as it had been explained to me, is a reference to the man who cheats with someone's wife when her husband is out of town. "Wet," as I'm certain I don't need to tell readers, also has unsavory associations in Chicano parlance. The flavors and textures of the Wet Sancho were in keeping with the aroma of the fast-food restaurant's interior.

Inflections of this ambivalence toward the cultural nuances of Mexican and Chicano culture are found throughout the Midwest. Founded in Minnesota in 1975 by Marno McDermott and former Green Bay Packers player Max McGee, the restaurant chain Chi-Chi's provided the Midwest region with the blueprint for a midwestern idea about Mexican food and presentation, complete with festive puns: in 2001, the chain applied for a trademark on the word "salsafication," but it was denied by the Trademark Trial and Appeal Board. At the height of its powers, there were 210 full-service restaurants in Illinois, Indiana, Maryland, Michigan, Ohio, Pennsylvania, Virginia, and Wisconsin.[1] The "fiesta" atmosphere made it a family destination for midwesterners, who apparently had no idea that the restaurant's name in Spanish was slang for "tits." Special occasions, particularly birthdays, brought out the sombrero and a crowd of clapping servers who concluded their serenade with a thunderous "Olé!"[2] In 2003 the

Figure 1. Chi-Chi's restaurant.

chain experienced financial crisis, which was generally attributed to its pace of growth coupled with the success of its competitors in the arena of casual, sit-down dining with full bar service, but the coffin's final nail came from one of the century's most significant hepatitis A outbreaks, linked to the green onions at one of the Chi-Chi's locations. By September 2004, Chi-Chi's closed all of its remaining restaurants in North America.[3] The recipes and brand-name products still exist, such as the one for their queso (regionally pronounced "kay-so") dip:

> 1 pound Velveeta cheese
> ¾ teaspoon granulated garlic
> 4 ½ ounces canned diced green chilies, drained
> ¾ ounce canned diced jalapeño, drained
> ¾ ounce fresh diced green pepper
> 2 ¾ ounces canned red peppers, diced and drained
>
> Cut processed cheese into chunks no more than 1 inch thick. Spread cheese pieces evenly in the bottom of a microwavable dish large enough for all ingredients. Spread all remaining ingredients evenly over the top of the processed cheese. Cover with a microwavable plastic lid and microwave on high for 2 minutes. Stir. Repeat the microwave process and stirring process until melted. Serve with your favorite tortilla chips.

As a representation of Mexican culinary practices, the Chi-Chi's restaurant chain stages a brand of Mexicanness that combines fantasy, south-of-the-border, carnival atmospherics with ultraprocessed foods that came to make up 70 percent of the American diet since the nineteenth century's invention of canning.

I am using the expression "culinary brownface" to compare this type of dining experience to the repertoires of nineteenth-century blackface minstrelsy, a form of entertainment that reached its height in the 1840s through the 1860s in which mostly White, mostly male performers blackened their faces with burnt cork and painted an exaggerated swath of white lip color to produce caricatured portrayals of enslaved African Americans. According to Rachel Sussman, this deprecating theatrical institution was not an attempt at a realistic representation of Black culture but rather a White appropriation of plantation and urban life interpreted from behind a mask, which worked to naturalize and sediment racist perceptions of Blacks as national truths.[4] My findings related to restaurant establishments in the Midwest result in an observable analogue between the nineteenth-century theatrical and the twenty-first-century gastronomic performances of ethnicity.

Before examining the particular kind of Mexican dining experiences in demand in restaurants of the Midwest, a geographic context is needed. Both Lima, Ohio, and Terre Haute, Indiana, have experienced declining industry since the mid-twentieth century due to a variety of factors, such as the transfer of manufacturing to other parts of the United States, increased automation, the decline of the U.S. steel and coal industries, neoliberal policies such as NAFTA, and outsourcing. Meanwhile, the greater region has witnessed a growth in Mexican residents, with an estimated 10 percent of the United States' Mexican population now living in the Midwest. Heritage food practices play a stabilizing role in the adjustment process of peoples experiencing the consequences of geographic and social displacement, even as migrants frequently own, staff, and perform exaggerated ethnicity in the brownface establishments I investigate below.

A working-class city in northern Ohio, in 2013 the average household income in Lima was $28,186 a year, against the national average of $53,000.[5] In October 2014, Janet Reitman's article in *Rolling Stone* magazine titled "Where the Tea Party Rules" describes the University of Vermont's 2013 urbanism study that names Lima, "whose steadily declining population now stands at roughly 38,000, as one of the country's 'saddest' cities, just behind Memphis, Tennessee, and Flint, Michigan."[6] With its refinery complex constituting one of the largest sources of chemical pollution in the northeastern region of the country, disproportionately high rates of cancer are coupled with upside-down mortgages, so that many who might otherwise pursue opportunities in other regions find themselves immobilized by negative equity. In popular culture the Fox network television series *Glee* (2009–15) contributed the phrase "Lima loser" to the national lexicon, referring to a person that would never amount to anything in life, or, simply put, a person that would never leave Lima. The recent racial demographics show that Lima's composition is 67 percent Caucasian, 26 percent Black or African American, and 3 percent Hispanic or Latino.[7]

Terre Haute, Indiana, approximately an hour and fifteen minutes' drive west from state capital Indianapolis, was famous for its Indiana State University graduate and Boston Celtic's star Larry Bird during the 1980s, but this distinction now goes to the county's methamphetamine epidemic. In July 2015, an *IndyStar* headline read "Indiana Meth Lab Capital Has No Challengers,"[8] and in 2014 the *Tristate* also announced the state's peerless distinction when it announced "Indiana Crowned Meth Capital of United States."[9] In the Vigo County Jail, where Terre Haute is located, 73 percent of the inmate population is held for meth-related charges.[10] The city's 2014 population was reported at 60,956 by the U.S. Census Bureau; an estimated median household income was reported to be $30,244 in 2013. The 2000 census reported White residents to compose 86.26 percent of the general population, with African American constituting 9.77 percent, and Latinos making up a little less than 2 percent.[11] The birthplace of Eugene Debs (1855–1926), famed for opposing Woodrow Wilson as the Socialist Party candidate in the 1912 Presidential Election and elected to an Indiana congressional seat in 1916 on a pacifist platform ahead of the First World War, in 2012 Indiana became the rust belt's first state to pass the "right-to-work" bill's powerful, antiunion legislation. Joseph J. Varga's "Breaking the Heartland: Creating the Precariat in the US Lower Rust Belt" explains how the decomposition of the bargaining power of the region's wageworkers have brought about a "precariat," or a new, more precarious class of workers that is changing the social landscape of the heartland.[12] Only two cities in Indiana reported greater job losses than Terre Haute. Robert Guell and Kevin Christ remark: "One need not have lived in Indiana for 25 years to know that the three most economically troubled metro areas since the 1990s have been Kokomo, Muncie and Terre Haute."[13]

Given the low numbers of heritage eaters in the population when compared with the high demand and distribution of Mexican food establishments in the rust belt region, the notion of the "contact zone" developed by Mary Louise Pratt is particularly useful to our understanding of how geographically separated peoples come into contact and establish relations, while preserving the circumstances of racial inequality and conflict. According to Pratt, a "contact" perspective "emphasizes how subjects are constituted in and by their relations to each other . . . not in terms of separateness or apartheid, but in terms of copresence, interaction, interlocking understandings and practices, often within radically asymmetrical relations of power."[14] It is necessary to bear in mind that the Mexican food preparations geared toward Anglo consumers examined in this chapter are not the result of geographic and culinary transplantation but rather the fruits of asymmetrical relations that privilege Anglo understandings and expectations about Mexican food as another realm where conquest is reproduced and performed.

As explored in the previous chapter's definition of Mexican cooking, Zilkia Janer finds two distinct types of dietary approaches characterizing Mexican dining in the states. For peoples of Mexican descent, eating habits may remain kin to the foodways of compatriots on the other side of the border: a testament to the migratory patterns, geographic proximity, and availability of popular ingredients native to Mexico. While the greater Lima area could claim one establishment that was by and for people of Mexican origin, the overwhelming Mexican food experience in both cities featured another style, which is characterized by contact-zone adaptation to Anglo norms and preferences, along with the cultural and geographic distancing from heritage products and flavors.[15] Arellano adds a third line of gastronomic development, which is the fast-food chain's imprint on U.S. perceptions of Mexican cuisine.[16] In the first chapter, I also argue for the consideration of Mexican fine dining as a fourth column in Mexican gastronomy, with a new emphasis shared by both chefs and diners on locally and sustainably produced ingredients.

In the Midwest, examples of all four categories of Mexican eateries thrive. My personal experience gleaned from a seven-year stint living in Chicago's predominantly Mexican Pilsen community offered a diversity of choices representing Mexican-based dietary norms and preferences, where taquerías offered traditional fare on comal-warmed tortillas de maíz made in house or from one of the two local tortillerías. Steaming corn tortillas heaped with cabeza (a mixture of meats from the head of a cow), lengua (beef tongue), and birria (shredded goat meat) are topped with cilantro, lime, and chopped onions. The ground beef, shredded iceberg lettuce, sour cream, and grated cheddar cheese lining a Taco Bell hard shell ("Nothing beats the snap and crunch of these great Taco Bell Crunchy Taco Shells," according to the Walmart web advertisement for the Taco Bell 12-count box) bears no resemblance to the tacos offered in Pilsen's heritage-style diners. Viewed as a total region, heritage eating thrives in Chicago and in other areas of the Midwest where migratory patterns and Mexican-dominant neighborhoods allow for an expansive market for home-style cuisine as well as contemporary and imaginative innovations based on the same. In the rust belt context of Mexican dishes that I analyze here, where economic crisis and scant exposure to cultural diversity reign, I am specifically focused on the restaurants that have been adapted to conform to Anglo demand for Mexican fare at reasonable prices in casual, sit-down dining environments.

Adaptive Authenticity: Midwest Mex

Blackface minstrelsy was built on repertoires of Whites performing Blackness who had little understanding of the performances and customs they observed. They would then, by isolating and reproducing these behaviors and musical practices, develop a catalog that best suited their own desires and the desires of their audiences. With little context for what they were seeing and an uncritical relationship to Black realities and racial oppression, blackface minstrels donned a demeaning mask but also insisted that the mask was an "authentic" representative of its referent. However, Zora Neale Hurston has pointed out a specific irony of White interpretations of Black cultural expressions that is relevant to our understanding of brownface: the Whites were often observing, and then imitating, performances that were, in fact, Black imitations of White culture.[17] An example is the "cake walk," that began as a Black imitation of movements witnessed at White balls. This fabric of misinterpreted parodies of Whites by Blacks then became the "truth" for audiences that propagated the myth of Blacks as moronic and docile, capable of breaking into spontaneous violence over a watermelon, and blissfully content in their roles as slaves.

The marketing of authenticity is remarked by Krishnendu Ray, chair of the Nutrition and Food Studies Department at New York University and author of the new book *The Ethnic Restaurateur* (2016). He explains that what "authentic" means is, in reality, a replica, or a "true copy of our expectations," that has come to epitomize what a dish should taste like, which then informs how immigrant cooks must couch their offerings.[18] These notions imposed by nonheritage, Midwest consumers on the ethnic Other's diets then become the norm, the standard to which all dishes are held. Of course, today's restaurant trends favoring local, seasonal, and regional ethnic cuisines are associated with affluence, and only global elites with ready access to air travel and exposure to a wide variety of foodsheds could accountably weigh in on how "real" a plate of tacos is. For the working-class residents of Lima and Terre Haute, Mexican restaurants constitute the principle, and arguably the most thriving, casual, sit-down dining experience available on a budget: a post-NAFTA, prairie type of cosmopolitanism. And the bulk of the residents, as is the case with low- and middle-income people elsewhere in the nation, could easily qualify as victims of, rather that accomplices to, the Standard American Diet (the SAD diet), or the Western pattern diet that is characterized by higher intakes of red and processed meat, high-fructose corn syrup, high-fat dairy products, processed and refined grains, hydrogenated fats, and fried foods that inevitably contribute to autoimmune and inflammatory diseases as well as cancer and cardiovascular disease. So I am not suggesting that the tendency across the restaurants I visited to serve enchiladas bathed in a red puree that tastes more like spaghetti sauce than salsa constitutes a form of calculated racial oppression in the vein of the blackface minstrel show. Quite the contrary—I firmly stand behind the principle that people should be able to interpret and modify recipes in the ways that best suit them. But such Mexican restaurants—in their food preparations, interior designs, and marketing materials—are not imitations of Mexican eating and dining conventions but rather, like with minstrelsy, imitations of the Mexican imitation of Western dining.

The vast array of clichés and stereotypes surrounding Midwest Mexican food presentations suggests to consumers that they have crossed a cultural border into a new gastronomic geography, when in fact they are faithfully replicating a culinary framework based on Taco Bell and Chi-Chi's. As Gustavo Arellano notes, Taco Bell often defines Anglo experiences with Mexican food.[19] Originating in Irvine, California, this company began in 1962 by Glen Bell, who loosely based his recipes on the fried, hand-rolled taquitos served in Olvera Street's historical Cielito Lindo food stand located on Olvera Street in Los Angeles since the 1930s. Their style of frying corn tortillas for their tacos was imitated broadly in the Los Angeles region, and today's Taco Bell company now has 6,500 locations in all 50 states, selling more than 2 billion tacos each year. According to Jeffrey Pilcher, author of *Planet Taco: A Global History of Mexican Food*, the Taco Bell chain helped popularize Mexican food in a country that had previously viewed the neighboring country's cuisine with disdain.[20] Restaurants in Lima and Terre Haute and elsewhere in the Midwest where Mexican food is featured almost universally assign the "authentic" designation to their food because (and not in spite of the fact that) it is based on the Taco Bell and Chi-Chi's genealogy of ingredients and preparations. And the dishes most central to Midwest Mexican menus favored by the Taco Bell and Chi-Chi's franchises are thoroughly made in the United States, usually representing variants on Arizonan, Californian, or Texan interpretations of Mexican fare that were adapted to attract European American consumers.

We'll start with what might be the most popular main course item in the two cities that I visited, corroborated by personal interviews with cooks, by observations in dining rooms, and from the ubiquity of the dish across the menus examined. The chimichanga, according to Marc Lacey's *New York Times* article "Arizonans Vie to Claim Cross-Cultural Fried Food" (2011), a deep fried burrito that can be stuffed with beef, pork, chicken, or fish, and is typically served under generous portions of mild sauce and cheese or melted processed cheese food, does not appear in any Spanish-language dictionaries, but might be translated roughly as "thingamajig." "But Mexicans do not tend to embrace the chimi as their own, even though chimichangas can be found on menus in northern Mexico, usually as chivechangas."[21] Appearing in restaurants in the 1950s, several Arizonan restaurants lay claim to its invention. I personally recall my Chihuahua-born grandmother, who was raised in Arizona from the time of her infancy, frying slim burritos stuffed into oversized flour tortillas with refried beans and chorizo. The burritos were chopped into three sections to make a finger food that was served at all family gatherings, where a punch bowl heaped high with them would quickly be emptied. Later, when I made a vegetarian version of this indispensable appetizer, it was always a first for Mexican and Chicano friends who had seldom experienced a fried burrito that was roughly the size of an egg roll.

And the margarita is the child of Larry Cano, owner of El Torito Grill in Encino, California, with an eye toward the well-heeled neighbors who wanted a Mexican dinner suitable for the executive class. Specifically targeting the women who wanted to enjoy the frozen daiquiri's celebratory appearance and feminine aesthetic, Cano invented the margarita: a daiquiri served with tequila instead of rum. He made it for two young women who had just received a bonus at work. The next time they came in, they asked for it again.[22] The burrito as we know it—the Chipotle-style, flour tortilla rolled tightly around two days' worth of food—was born in San Francisco's Mission District in the 1960s when Febronio Ontiveros wanted to create a lunch food for the local Anglo workers that could rival the ease and speed of the sandwich. He had eaten burritos in his youth in the northern Mexican state of Durango, where burritos were the humble lunch of manual laborers, the contents usually consisting of whatever leftovers the home's larder could provide. Ontiveros transformed this working-class, northern Mexican food into an American institution when he went to a tortilla factory and requested that they create a much larger version of the flour tortilla in order to create a hearty main course. By the 1980s the San Francisco–style burrito and assembly line was a California institution, copied by San Francisco native Mike Mercer in the viral Chipotle chain beginning in 1995.[23]

And the genealogies go on. Fajitas, referring originally to a cut of steak around the cow's diaphragm and morphing into sizzling platters of just about anything, are from the Rio Grande Valley of Texas and became a trend at sit-down restaurants in the United States in the

1980s;[24] V-shaped fried taco shells are from California, and the cheese dip that is exceedingly popular in Midwest cities (used as an appetizer dip or to smother burritos and nachos) is a Texas mainstay that was historically made with Mexican Asadero, Manchego, or Chihuahua cheeses and known as queso fundido, and transformed by the flavors of various brands of processed white and yellow products that FDA regulations will not allow to be called cheese.

In Yelp reviews in both Lima and Terre Haute, "authentic," "cheap," and "fast," are the most sought-after categories in casual Mexican dining, and reviewers who have spent time in the Southwest, such as Texas or Arizona, will evoke their travels to these parts in order to boast their culinary authority in all matters Mexican. But even reviewers who report zero hours in the Southwest or Mexico make confident claims as to their favorite eatery's authenticity. About the newly popular restaurant El Cazador in Lima, Yelpers enthuse:

> SAM B.: Great Great place!!!Huge menu with great authentic food! Enjoy you won't believe the food for a very reasonable price!
>
> BROTHER O.: Not only the best Mexican restaurant in Lima but the best restaurant in Lima period. Great food, great service, clean, authentic, full of light, and did I mention the food![25]

In order to be able to recommend a Mexican dining establishment, the patrons of Lima and Terre Haute's Mexican options must declare that the food is authentic. Lima's popular restaurant chain La Charreada (locally called "La Shuh-ray-duh"), writes on its website: "La Charreada takes pride in providing Lima with the freshest and truest of authentic Mexican food." Housed in the building formerly occupied by Chi-Chi's, La Charreada West's landing page shows photos of beef enchiladas smothered in "kay-so" accompanied by a pile of French fries, an appetizer dish of melted queso, a cheese-drenched plate of chicken fajitas, and a dining room decorated with large cartoon images of a brown child in an outsized sombrero who rides and then chases after a burro. In the photo of La Charreada West, the dining room is packed with patrons who, with the exception of one African American patron, are entirely Anglo in appearance. A young man, the only person of mestizo appearance in the frame, serves platters of food with a serious expression on his face. Exhibiting the most significant characteristic of culinary brownface, food practices representing the Western pattern diet come with assurances of their cultural legitimacy in an Anglo-facing staging of ethnicity.

In the ten restaurants I visited in both cities, chimichangas, faji-tas, taco plates, processed cheese food, and margaritas exemplified the fare that customers lauded as "authentic," even though the flavors and ingredients were universally geared toward nonheritage consumption. Processed cheese food oozed out of chiles rellenos; gobs of sour cream, heaps of iceberg lettuce, and shredded American cheese were piled onto V-shaped hard-shell tacos, and although the genealogies of these foods are easily traced to mestizo imitation of Anglo dietary styles, the notion of authenticity remains a pervasive concept across these establishments, epitomizing the tendency to push the limits of this term beyond its coherence as a descriptor. In fact, Russell Cobb begins his volume *The Paradox of Authenticity in a Globalized World* (2014) with, "There is no way to begin this section without thanking the hundreds of Mexican restaurants around the world who bill themselves as selling 'authentic Mexican food.' The original idea for this project came from a conversation about fish tacos, and whether something served with mayonnaise could ever be considered authentically Mexican."[26] Tracing the etymology to its Greek root *authentikos*, which denotes that which is pure, authoritative, and original, the postmodern high level of tolerance for cultural relativity is trumped by the quest for the allusive zest of authenticity, never mind that most of this hunt is informed by clever marketing schemes and unscrupulous hucksters. "We may not understand all the modes of production and distribution behind our food, our art, or our culture," writes Cobb, "but we want it to be *real*. How will we know what that is? We will simply have to believe that we will know it when we see it" (Cobb, 8). Such is the insistence on this word in the marketing of Mexican food that, unlike the attempts at certifications and other controls exerted by, say, the stewards of Louisiana creole cuisine, French champagne, and Mexican tequila, this constitutes an entirely futile claim. And yet, the word "authentic" clings to almost every conversation that non-Mexicans have about their favorite Mexican restaurants, because it means that they are doing a thing "right": they are not fooled by lesser "untrue" stagings of ethnic food and can boast an understanding of the authoritative versions of their favorite cuisine.

But culinary brownface is also *staffed* in a way that evokes the history of blackface performances. In minstrelsy, free and enslaved Blacks with little power to create their own interpretations and imagery in the popular musical traditions, invested their own talents and musical idioms in minstrel productions, as they provided one of the few venues for artistic publication and professionalization. Mexican cooks and servers in brownface dining establishments have a qualitatively safer space in which their own mestizaje may be exhibited without being thought of as "matter out of place"—a national contaminant that political and popular discourses dream of eliminating through increased border security and aggressive deportation policies. Whether it be grinning and dancing and doing a soft shoe, or clapping out a happy sombrero birthday serenade, Latino owners of and employees in brownface establishments do more than perform customer service—they also perform Anglo ideas about ethnicity to champion the "fiestafication" legacy of Midwestern Chi-Chi's and Taco Bell chains.

Perhaps the most significant measure of the gustatory distance from Mexican flavors and ingredients came from conversations with the Mexican staff. At La Charreada West, the Spanish-speaking server told me that he only liked to eat "real" Mexican food, and would travel to other cities or visit a taquería called Lucero's, located about thirty minutes away, when he wanted to eat out. In Terre Haute, I interviewed Magali Mireles, bartender of Agave Vintage Cocktails, whose family hails from Oaxaca. She made a business in the rust belt from selling homemade mole, tamales, gorditas, flautas, and her signature tres leches cake to the kitchen and wait staff of the city's Mexican restaurants, delivering food to their workplace in brownface establishments where they found the food to be inedible.

Another telling example of how the cuisine was staged for Anglos was found at Terre Haute's Real Hacienda, a restaurant that has six locations in Terre Haute and its vicinity. When my son ordered tacos de carne asada in Spanish, the server brought him the Mexican-style soft tacos with cilantro and onion, while at the table next to us, he had delivered crispy, Taco Bell–style tacos to a table of Anglo construction workers. Intrigued, I questioned the server about how he indicated to the cook which way the menu item was to be prepared. "Do you have a code," I inquired, "like 'TP' for 'taco paisano' on the ticket for the cook?" He, along with the two other Spanish-speaking servers in the vicinity who happened to overhear my query, giggled at this notion. "I just tell the cook to put on cilantro and cebolla," he explained. The cook understood from the ingredients requested which style of taco he was to prepare. And so I learned that an adaptive culinary bilingualism thrives in these spaces that seldom see heritage diners in the front of the house as customers, but will make accommodations based on their knowledge of two separate foodways that share the same names. What I refer to as adaptive authenticity comes from my observations about the constant adjustment of the "true" and "authoritative" versions of a dish—claims on which Anglo patrons assert and rely—while heritage diners create different versions that they prepare and serve for themselves and diners that share their culinary referents about what is, and is not, palatable.

Cabo Wabo and the Speedy Gonzalez Combo Plate: Eating the Exotic Other

Johnston and Baumann submit that the neocolonial "desire to eat the exotic Other" may represent an impetus for intercultural exchange and the broadening of the culinary canon beyond Euro-American cuisine.[27] While this might be the case for establishments that do not actively rely on cultural stereotypes, brownface establishments exaggerate carnivalesque and bordertown lawlessness to encourage sales. Charles Ramirez Berg draws a parallel between Edward Said's Orientalism and "Latinism," describing the discursive process of stereotypical mass media representations of Latinos as the construction of Latin Americans and U.S. Latinx in a manner that justifies United States' imperialistic goals.[28] The exotic Other, in the restaurants visited, bear the imprint of specific colonial impulses that, in brownface restaurants, tend to be coded as a Mexican celebration of moral decadence in keeping with sex-and-booze-crazed spring breaks in Cancun and overindulgence on Cinco de Mayo. Cabo Wabo provides a particularly infamous example of the colonial construction of Mexican debauchery. Sammy Hagar, the occasional singer of the band Van Halen since 1985, opened a large bar and restaurant in Cabo San

Lucas (nicknamed "Cabo," which means "cape"). Taking the town's nickname Cabo, he added a shortened version of the word "wobble" ("Wabo") after reportedly seeing a man walk unsteadily on the beach after a night of drinking: the Cabo wobble.

At Lima's Bandido's restaurant, the oldest Mexican restaurant in the town, their slogan "better than authentic" hovers over their entrance. First, the name. From 1967 to 1971, Frito Bandito was the cartoon mascot for the Frito Lay corn chip brand. Mel Blanc, who voiced the other famous character of the era Speedy Gonzales, used an exaggerated, Speedy-esque "Mexican" accent. The Frito Bandito spoke broken English and robbed people of their prized Fritos snack, referencing the stereotype of Mexican banditry in film and popular media. Pressure from the National Mexican-American Anti-Defamation Committee forced Frito Lay to update to the character, so they removed his gold tooth and shaved his beard stubble, and finally retired the character in 1971.

Bandido's was reviled by a couple that I spoke with in Lima, and is panned in several consumer reviews online, although the food there did not seem to be any worse than that from the other brownface restaurants that I visited. However, there seemed to be an understanding that their reliance on ethnic stereotypes was not only out-of-date for the restaurant but out-of-date for the town. Not only are there no claims to authenticity, but there are no people of Mexican or mestizo appearance employed in the front or back of the house, and we loudly heard a server comment that she didn't speak Spanish when someone asked her a menu-related question.

Under new management, their emphasis on fresh ingredients and their "build your own burrito" shows a shift away from the combo plates approach that has organized brownface menus for decades and a move toward Chipotle as the new standard for marketing and presentation. Notably, the Speedy Gonzalez Combo Plate (taco, enchilada, and choice of rice or beans) was featured on every menu in Lima and also found in Terre Haute, but was not on the menu at Bandido's. However, at Bandido's they offer a food item called Jimmiechangas, as well as monthly low-price drink specials in an event they call "Cinco de Drinko." Cinco de Mayo is excluded from this event, presumably because it is a high-flow day for their patrons who will come in without the additional lure of special promotions. The artwork includes

Figure 2. Bandido's: Better than Authentic. Photo by author.

the sombreros, serapes, and tropical colors that typify the brownface dining room design; paintings of a very debauched Sancho Panza accompanying a very dizzy Don Quijote; and a series of desert images in which a solemn couple migrates across a lonely expanse of wilderness while clutching an inordinate number of balloons.

Although I was not unhappy when it came time to wind down our culinary tour of Lima's Mexican restaurants, it also must be emphasized that culinary brownface takes place not only in the Midwest but also, as evinced by Sammy Hagar, well within Mexican national territory wherever ethnic stereotypes are exploited to market Mexican cooking for Western consumers. It must also be noted that heritage cooking thrives in many places in the Midwest, and Lima is not an exception. Lima's La Charreada employee recommended we go to Lucero's in nearby Ottawa for heritage cooking that he felt best represented his culture's food preparation. The modest, clean taquería was decorated with murals on the inside and out in an aesthetic that recalled the Chicano and Mexican proletarian public art movements. Upon speaking Spanish with the owner, he proudly showed us around

Figure 3. Lucero restaurant interior. Photo by author.

his store and restaurant, informing us that a teacher from Columbus, Ohio, traveled all the way to Ottawa to visit his restaurant. After
spending so much time in serape- and sombrero-driven dining rooms
with menus boasting Speedy Gonzales combo plates, the energy felt
palpably different: no one was performing cartoon versions of ethnicity for Whites.

Postdata: Columbus Effect, Columbus, Ohio

While this chapter has been concerned with the specificities of Mexican restaurants in the two cities of Lima, Ohio, and Terre Haute, Indiana, the tale of my Odyssean homecoming would be incomplete without mention of my visit to Cosecha . . . Columbus. We've already seen that the Cosecha of Oakland was founded by chef and proprietor Dominica Rice-Cisneros in 2011. We also discussed how the Columbus Effect, as remarked by Maria Elena Cepeda, describes the process by which people of European descent grant the importance of "discovery" to their own repackaging and control of Latin American cultural production when it serves their interests.[29]

Fresh repackaging is one of the selling points for Columbus's version of the Oakland restaurant. Listed as one of "The 12 Hottest New Restaurants in Columbus, Ohio," by *Eater* in June 2017, journalists and social media commentators invariably share their admiration for the chic interior.[30] Set in the up-and-coming Italian Village neighborhood, Cocina Cosecha's high-end, rustic styling comes from its location in a rehabbed former dairy barn with concrete floors; high, beamed ceilings and industrial brick walls; spacious patio; and what one reviewer referred to as "understated decorations that reference Mexican landscape and culture."[31] The price point and the "understated" Mexican references in the reviews seemed written to assure diners that Cosecha Columbus would provide a luxe and hip dining experience—a "new" way to enjoy Mexican flavors.

The twenty-something-year-old-chef Silas Caeton, who has so far been associated with Mediterranean and Italian cooking, began to explore Mexican cooking in 2014 when he made a ten-day trip to the country. Nevertheless, one journalist claims that his personal history amply prepares him for a career in Mexican cuisine based on the fact that his father took pre-med courses in Guadalajara and became fluent in Spanish. "Dr. Caeton is fluent in Spanish, and his son has picked up the language, as well as his love of the country. This makes for a natural transition into his upcoming role as executive chef at Cosecha Cocina, which translates to 'Harvest' in Spanish." Citing Rick Bayless as his inspiration, he makes no claim to "authenticity" but rather focuses on blending Mexican cuisine with "modern techniques."[32]

Although the Columbus Effect is not so obvious in Caeton's own assertions of culinary mastery (aside from the mention of Rick Bayless), they are at the heart of what journalists claim he is providing for the city as well as in the vision that owner Chris Crader holds for his establishment. However, some Columbus residents are taking stock of the number of higher-end restaurants that serve Mexican-inspired cooking in Anglo-facing businesses. In a Facebook post dated April 2, 2017, by Sonya Fix, Department Head of ESL at Columbus College of Art and Design, she voices her concern about Crader's model from a citywide perspective:

> The space in Italian Village was beautiful and the food was aiight, but a restaurant touting authentic Mexican food with a white American owner with a white American chef felt like violence. I know this sentiment may appear overly dramatic and hyperbolic because ostensibly, Mexican food has been appropriated and co-opted in the U.S. for decades. But stay with me. Cosecha is emblematic of a particular type of violent erasure that occurs when authenticity is packaged and purveyed for a predominately white moneyed customer base by whites. The owner Chris Crader (of the Grow restaurant group) is quoted in ColumbusUnderground.com as saying "I just felt like nobody was taking that type of food seriously." Is Crader aware of the explosion of legitimately-authentic, amazing Mexican food being offered at restaurants and food trucks, owned and prepared by Mexican members of our community . . . which are breathing new life into communities. They are made possible due to immigrants from Mexico and Central America. And they take the authentic food they serve very seriously. . . . But choosing to get your "authentic" Mexican food from a gringo who touts local partnerships—but who doesn't appear to have partnered with the culinary talent and entrepreneurship within the Columbus Mexican community at all in his venture—wreaks a particular sort of economic violence, a closed loop of development via white privilege. Something that Columbus is really good at.[33]

Fix's attention to Crader's "nobody was taking this food seriously" strikes a particular chord for Fix, who mentions several of the city's Latino-owned restaurants and provides links to several taco trucks that are located in many Columbus neighborhoods.

Oakland chef Rice-Cisneros became aware of an Ohio restaurant using the name Cosecha in 2016. The rustic chic style and the farm-to-table ethos that are also associated with Cosecha's Oakland dining space are now quite popular in the restaurant world, but it struck her as strange that the exact same font she has used since 2011 on Cosecha marketing materials was also used at Crader's new restaurant. Also, the Spanish syntax is odd. Cocina Rosa, for example, would translate into "pink kitchen," not "kitchen belonging to a woman named Rosa," since the modifier follows the noun in Spanish. Plenty of restaurants are called "cocina," but this word is followed by the name of the person the kitchen belongs to (Cocina de la Abuela, for example, would translate to Grandma's Kitchen). "Mercado de la cosecha" or "fiesta de la cosecha" ("harvest market" or "feast of the harvest") are current usages of the word "harvest" that make sense in the Spanish language, but Crader's choice of title reveals little knowledge of Spanish and little effort in learning about the conventions of Mexican restaurant identities. Cosecha is a highly unusual name for a restaurant in the Mexican context (a web search reveals only the two, nationally). Crader's "nobody was taking it seriously," in the wake of his obvious need to copy people who obviously *were*, is the kind of hubris that, as Fix words it in her post, reflects the "closed loop of development via white privilege."

Even so, Rice-Cisneros encouraged me to become a Cocina Cosecha patron, "if it meets a need." She believes firmly that nonheritage restaurateurs who partner with and/or feature the talents of heritage chefs and recipes can be extremely beneficial for the prospects of Mexican cuisine and its professionals. Recently featured as a presenter at the Foro Mundial de la Gastronomía Mexicana in Mexico City (October 2017) as part of the panel "Mexicanas cocinando en California," Rice-Cisneros joins her fellow heritage chefs in the call for more conversation around the people and foodsheds that make highly profitable recipes possible.[34] How are the owners constructively attributing their recipes and inspirations to the chefs and home cooks who have been creating Mexican menus for centuries? What are the ingredients that will help heritage foodsheds maintain their biodiversity? It's the lack of attribution—treating culinary traditions like found objects rather than intellectual property, and treating agricultural traditions like mineral wealth to be extracted and removed—that characterizes the "double" Columbus Effect.

As my last Midwest restaurant stop of this study, my visit to Crader's Cosecha, although touted as "understated rustic-chic" and described as "authentic," was firmly entrenched in the kind of brownface ethos so popular in Terre Haute and Lima. I sat directly underneath a large format print of Don Quijote riding a burro into a desertscape of the Southwest. Serapes and beer cozies were being sold from behind a counter. The chile relleno was full of undercooked rice and gooey cheddar cheese, and the poblano pepper's seeds had not been removed (when I pointed this out to the server, she said that was the customary preparation). The dark red substance that covered the enchilada and chile relleno was a thick, smoky chipotle paste that tasted more like southern barbeque sauce than anything that a Mexican kitchen might produce. In other words, slightly less blatant brownface in the décor did not equal less blatant brownface in the recipes.

Fix's comments reveal a large-scale problem in Columbus's Anglo-facing Mexican restaurants that tend toward heavy misappropriation, when they are not flatly racist. The restaurant chain Local Cantina, for example, has three locations around the city. Their logo is a large, black moustache, and signs hanging from the ceiling inexplicably read "sucio bigote" (moustache dirty), "beer, bottoms up," and "bailar en el bigote" (dance in the moustache). My Odyssean homecoming revealed the same pervasive tendencies that dominate Mexican dining options in other parts of the rust belt, even though Columbus, located in Franklin County, is considered far more liberal than its more economically blighted neighbors. Crader's Columbus (Effect) Cosecha was the end of the eating tour, but not the end of the fight.

Chapter 3

HOMEGIRL CAFÉ

La Conciencia Mestiza as Culinary Counterstory

home·girl
/ˈhōmˌɡərl/
noun US *informal*
a young female acquaintance from one's own town or neighborhood, or from the
same social background.
(especially among urban black people) a female member of a peer group or gang.

DICTIONARY.COM

Reclaiming Aberrant Identities

In May 2017 I took a tour at Homegirl Café, where we had two guides: a young man named Omar, who told us that he ran away from home at the age of fourteen, and his quiet trainee named Aurelio. Since 2007 Omar had cycled in and out of Homeboy Industries throughout his young adult years. We learned he had been shot seven times. He credited Homeboy Industries and its founder Father Gregory Boyle (Father Greg) with teaching him how to become a father, work with his rivals, and put the cycle of violence that defined his childhood and adolescence in his past. Shortly after gaining some seniority as a tour guide at Homeboy Industries, a homie from a rival gang was assigned to shadow Omar and learn how to lead tours and greet visitors. Thanks to Homeboy, he started to smile at former enemies and everyone else in the Homeboy community. Soon enough, "Everyone starts smiling and it's pretty freaky." Naturally, all five of us on Omar's tour replied with wide smiles of our own. Revealing traumatic experiences from his life in an uncomplicated, straightforward demeanor, Omar told us that leading these tours through the Homeboy Industries facilities and sharing his own story have been important aspects of his therapy.

I look around the group. My 1960s, cultural revolution–era, Nuyorican-turned-Chicano-movement mother, and three Anglo family members that I had acquired in the rust belt Midwest, who are impossible to imagine in the company of Black and Chicano tattooed felons until you see it firsthand. I was the only L.A. native, a Chicanarriqueña who had generally sported an artsy bent that would never have permitted me to be taken for a hardened chola in my youth. But they were always there. In my school, at the 7-Eleven and Ralphs supermarket, at the house parties that we attended or hosted, the danger and theatricality of these young girls was ever-present. Never to be caught without a riot of lip and eyeliner, they were at the center of the most interesting fights in the girls' bathroom or on the lawn of Water and Power in northeast L.A. And I recall as a teenager in the early '90s witnessing the ritual of a young girl in Lincoln Park being jumped into a gang by walking through a long corridor of members close to her in age. They took turns pummeling her until she was crawling on the ground, and then, satisfied with her submission, they lifted her up into their arms to welcome her to their fold. It was terrifying, but also jubilant: a living diorama of the Smile Now, Cry Later tattoo omnipresent among Chicanx and Latinx youth from hard neighborhoods.

As a pathway out of the cyclical torrents of mental health disease, addiction, abuse, and the alienations of poverty, sexism, and racism, the generative work of Homegirl Café, a full-service restaurant, and one of Homeboy Industries' most successful social enterprises, constitutes a form of grassroots resistance to the expansion of the punishment industry that antiprison activist Angela Davis calls the "prison industrial complex." Interpreted here as a culinary expression of la conciencia mestiza (Anzaldúa, Sandoval), the spatial and social configuration of the café provides a pipeline away from corrections and into self-determination that draws from, rather than preaches against, street-identified Chicana subject formation. My "Chola vs. Chiquita bananas" section considers the image of the homegirl, or chola, as the central referent of Homegirl Café. By reclaiming the chola figure as a model for community empowerment, Homegirl Café provides an alternative mediatization of mestiza womanhood, countering food advertising stereotypes such as the Chiquita bananas and Abuelita chocolate logos that either eroticize Latin American agricultural products through the styling of the Latina body or brand culinary authenticity as that which is located south of the U.S.-Mexico border.

Next, my "Provider vs. Pathogen" section discusses how the restaurant and its trainees have created a new matrix of meaning associated with barrio-identified women that aligns them with food provisioning, thus defying nativist visions of homegirls as parasites, pathogens, and/or superpredators. Through their locations in city hall and the Los Angeles International Airport, Homegirl Café celebrates local Latinas as providers at the forefront of the city's culinary innovation.

At the end of the millennium's second decade, we are entering a time in which even politically moderate analysts are beginning to recognize the need either for prison reform or prison abolition, marking a shift in attitudes toward mass incarceration that prevailed in the recent past. Although the upswing of large-scale incarceration related to the '80s-era War on Drugs and the political enthusiasm for harsher sentencing laws in the 1980s and 1990s are credited by conservative pundits as the reason behind the nation's falling crime rates, we know now that skyrocketing imprisonment of the domestic population is actually confirmed to have a negligible effect on the decline of crime.[1] With 2.2 million people incarcerated in the nation's prisons and jails, the United States holds the dubious distinction of being the world's leader in incarceration rates, which have swelled by 500 percent in the last four decades. Incarcerating 716 people for every 100,000 residents, the United States represents about 4.4 percent of the world's population, while being home to around 22 percent of the world's prison population.

Pointing out that national strategies of incarceration constitute a thinly veiled carry-over from human slavery, in 1997 antiprison activist Angela Davis claimed that the "prison industrial complex," or the for-profit, metastasizing penal system, targets populations contending with homelessness, unemployment, drug addiction, mental illness, and other problems that disappear from the public when correctional facilities serve to extract sub–minimum wage labor from detainees rather than promote their rehabilitation. With a message of hope amid a national atmosphere of growing conservatism and its rampant and dangerous criminalization of people of color, Davis exhorts grassroots organizers to resist the unchecked expansion of the punishment industry.

Considering the impressive number of grassroots projects that continue to resist the expansion of the punishment industry, it ought to be possible to bring these efforts together to create radical and nationally visible movements that can legitimize anti-capitalist critiques of the prison industrial complex. It ought to be possible to build movements in defense of prisoners' human rights and movements that persuasively argue that what we need is not new prisons, but new health care, housing, education, drug programs, jobs, and education. To safeguard a democratic future, it is possible and necessary to weave together the many and increasing strands of resistance to the prison industrial complex into a powerful movement for social transformation.[2]

The call to shift from incarceration to community-based prevention and treatment for substance abuse and the investment in interventions that promote youth development and age-appropriate, evidence-based responses to delinquency are central to Davis's vision that now thrives at Homegirl Café.

Developed to "divert" young people involved in delinquent acts from the more long-term and far-reaching outcomes of processing by adult criminal courts, diversion programs became popular in the 1960s to target various criminogenic factors associated with future incarceration. Widely acknowledged to be one of the largest and most successful gang-intervention, rehabilitation, and reentry programs in the country, Homeboy Industries programs include an emphasis on the mentorship, education, vocational skills, and personal responsibility that have been the key strategies in the reduction of recidivism rates since the '60s.[3] When Father Greg was sent to work at Dolores Mission in the mid-1980s, it was Los Angeles's poorest parish, which sat in the middle of Pico Gardens and Aliso Village, two of the country's largest public housing projects west of the Mississippi. Known for hosting the city's highest rates of gang activity, at the time of writing *Tattoos on the Heart* in 2010, Father Greg had been called on to bury 168 young people who had died from gang-related violence. Even in the neighborhoods where they were from, gang members were viewed as the enemy, until the persistent efforts of the Dolores Mission leadership developed an attitude and a series of interventions based on their faith practices that lead to another way of relating to delinquency in their parish precinct. They started with a small job program, Jobs for a Future, in Boyle Heights in 1988. Then in 1992 Ray Stark, a renowned Hollywood agent, purchased an old bakery across the street from the church, and Jobs for the Future became Homeboy Bakery, their first social enterprise. Two months later, they were making Homeboy Tortillas, and by 2001, Homeboy Industries had grown into an independent nonprofit organization.

Born in Guadalajara, Patricia Zarate became a resident of the Boyle Heights neighborhood and gave herself to the vision of the Dolores Mission, where her deep involvement in immigration advocacy at the Dolores Mission led to a job as Father Greg's assistant. Her unique cooking talents were soon noticed, and she lent her skills to the priests at the common house with an eclectic and healthy approach to Mexican cuisine. As a foundational force behind Homeboy Industries' programs and philosophy, Zarate's dedication to cooking grew with the program's needs, and, in 2005 Zarate's small Plaza Café in Boyle Heights was rechristened Homegirl Café.

Today, the entirety of Homegirl Café's proceeds benefits comprehensive intervention and wraparound services for thousands of former gang members who look to the café as both a sanctuary and an opportunity for reinvention. Forty-five women (and some men) are employed at Homegirl. While men who express interest in food service are welcome into the café's training program, the concentration of female employees in the same place allows Homeboy a successful way to address many issues specific to female participants, such as domestic violence, the skills needed to parent as a single mother, GED completion, and women's empowerment. Bearing the name of Homegirl Café in the city's Wholesale District in downtown Los Angeles, other food products are sold and distributed by the Homeboy Foods and Homeboy Bakery social enterprises, which operate with the café, but offer different training modules.

Homegirl Café's website reads: "Homegirl Café is a favorite farm-to-table breakfast and lunch spot featuring Latino flavors with a healthy, contemporary twist, where homegirls serve tables instead of serving time." With the restaurant, bakery, and urban farm offering comprehensive training programs to formerly incarcerated or high-risk men and women, the dining establishment offers what is often the first "real job" to many of its trainees. Providing an eighteen-month certificate program to high-risk and formerly gang-involved young women, Homegirl Café "flips the script" that has historically coidentified working-class Latinas with gang activity, detention, and dependency.

With its roots in the original Homeboy Bakery that started in 1992, the café's trajectory from a small, neighborhood nook to one of the city's culinary powerhouses, and its delicious disruption of the prison industrial complex, has deeper roots in the generative ritual of offering and receiving food. The seed life of the community transformation that culminates in Homegirl Café's impact begins with the Christian Base Communities / Comunidades Eclesiasticas de Base (CEBs) of the Dolores Mission parish east of downtown Los Angeles. Meeting weekly in small groups to study scripture and contemplate the Jesuit question of, "What is God asking us to do, here and now?" the strong female leadership of the CEBs have helped to steer the congregation toward fostering an ethos of service and compassion. The various nonprofit organizations that grew from the CEBs commitments to service are numerous, spanning to include Homeboy Industries, Proyecto Pastoral at Dolores Mission, CHIRLA, and the East Los Angeles Housing Coalition—no mean feat for a humble group of señoras in the most gang-plagued part of the metropolis. The women of the CEBs, led in Father Greg's early days by Teresa Navarro and Paula Hernandez, exhorted fellow parishioners to understand that gang members were not their enemy, but rather their sons and daughters—their kin and responsibility. Father Greg credits these parish leaders for making the Dolores Mission a safe haven for homies to congregate. One of the CEBs, the Comité pro Paz (Committee for Peace), not only united in a campaign for peace but also worked with Father Greg to organize Jobs for the Future, which advocated for the employment of youths involved in gang activity.

By drawing on their spiritual discipline to give Dolores Mission an identity that prioritized social justice, they created a transnational space for mestiza agency that honored the sacred in the daily lives of the most vulnerable members of the community and fully embraced the self that they recognized in the youths beleaguered by criminal convictions, gang affiliations, mental health problems, addictions, homelessness, and abuse: all of the circumstances that, as Davis notes, become erased by the phenomenon of mass incarcerations. The many-faced recognition of self in the plight of the sufferer opens the space of Chicana mestizaje, or the border-situated transformation of oppression into a sacred relationship with social justice. In the words of Gloria Anzaldúa's *Borderlands* (1981), the space of renewal comes from previously suppressed perspectives that include, rather than remove, the realm of abjection.

> I am cultureless because, as a feminist, I challenge the collective cultural/religious male-derived beliefs of Indo-Hispanics and Anglos; yet I am cultured because I am participating in the creation of yet another culture, a new story to explain the world and our participation in it, a new value system with images and symbols that connect us to each other and to the planet. *Soy un amasamiento*, an act of kneading, of uniting and joining that not only has produced both a creature of darkness and a creature of light, but also a creature that questions the definitions of light and dark and gives them new meaning. (80–81)

The significance of hybridity in Anzaldúa's meditations on Chicana identity constitutes a radical departure from the narrow recourse to nation-referencing mythologies that were prevalent during the civil rights and Chicano rights movement (1965–75). Emphasizing the re-evaluation of suppressed realms of knowledge to incorporate devalued bodies and faith expressions, Chicana mestizaje draws strength from myriad cultural exclusions and disjunctures as a site of creative transcendence (Pérez, Delgadillo). Food preparation at Homegirl Café, viewed here as a "new value system" that challenges patriarchal and colonial logics, forms the technology by which mestiza consciousness is transmitted.

The project of Chicana mestizaje is useful to understand what is radical, rather than merely liberal, about the positioning of Chicana working-class and otherwise marginalized women at Homegirl Café. Informed by Chela Sandoval's development of la conciencia mestiza, I refer to Chicana mestizaje, and alternately, borderlands feminism, as a form of consciousness that emphasizes transversions and crossings to erode the logic of patriarchal and colonial social orderings. Emphasizing the coalitional processes that arise out of the complexities of borderlands identities, Chicana mestizaje departs from other modes of resistance. Outlined in Sandoval's essay, modes of Chicano opposition include Chicana/o cultural nationalism that values cultural continuity over feminist transformative trajectories; Chicano separatism that prioritizes greater autonomy from—and alternatives to—mainstream values and institutions; Chicana liberalism that focuses on socioeconomic and cultural enfranchisement of Chicanas within existing institutions; and insurgent feminism that advocates for gender liberation as a condition of revolutionary transformation.[4] In dialogue with Anzaldúa, Sandoval sustains Sonia Saldivar-Hull's vision of Anzaldúa's "new mestiza consciousness" as the psyche's survival of a cultural crossroads that not only embodies and transcends cultural fragmentation but also creates new liberatory practices that arise out of the double consciousness that the mestiza experiences.[5] Born of decolonial and antisexist U.S. histories, Sandoval's U.S. Third World feminism—a mestiza or borderlands feminism—provides the critical apparatus for recognition and interpretation of the politics and expressive cultures of Chicanas and mestizas in the United States.[6]

Fulfilling Davis's vision (to whom Sandoval dedicates her essay) by establishing a grassroots coalition that addresses the multiple oppressions silenced by the prison industrial complex, Homegirl Café, at the same time, clears the way toward a feminist and decolonial space:

> Oppositional mestizaje occurs when the unexplored affinities inside of difference attract, combine, and relate new constituencies into a coalition of resistance: Any such generalized and politicized coalitional consciousness, however, can only occur on the site of a social movement that was once overlooked because it was perceived as limited, restricted by gender, sex, or race identity: U.S. third world feminism; a feminism developed by U.S. women of color and by Chicana feminists under the sign of "la conciencia de la mestiza."[7]

Occurring specifically "on the site of a social movement that was once overlooked," Homegirl Café anchors its identity and inspiration in the radical inclusion of the Chicanas, mestizas, and Latinas defined by barrio experience.

The women of the CEBs didn't just pass out fliers and make speeches. Nondiscursive persuasion happened in the form of carne asada gatherings, where traditional grilled meat and tortillas turned the gathered faithful into family. They hosted a Thanksgiving dinner for homies who did not have families to celebrate the holiday with. In the most gang-plagued corner of the city, the women upheld the dignity of even their most struggling of neighbors, in accordance with the commitment Father Greg has articulated as "meeting people where they are." Compare this to the current national sentiment regarding mestiza/o transnational families and youths: the current defense of the Deferred Action for Childhood Arrivals (DACA) reasons that good grades or military service deem an undocumented young person "worthy" of a dignified life on U.S. soil, but there should be no second chances. To allow that all the youth are the sons and daughters of the Dolores Mission parish, and not only the ones who had the sense—and privilege—to stay out of trouble, is conveyed by the ritual of welcoming all comers to be fed.

Today, the café serves as the architectural realization of the CEBs' work to advocate for the dignity of homies and homegirls. From local guests to international visitors, the café provides a space for the encounter between the diversion program participants and a public that may not otherwise enter into personal communication with youths and adults recovering from involvement in criminal activity and its many consequences. For guests, a border crossing into the vicarious experience of homie and homegirl struggles and hopes takes place—an enormous shift in consciousness. This shift is remarked in an early chapter in *G-dog* that describes a nurse who defended a young gang member who was hospitalized for critical gunshot injuries. Her coworkers were of the mind that, as a gangbanger, his injuries were simply what he deserved. The nurse came to the realization that she felt for the young man because she had spent time with him and had had the opportunity to observe and interact with the family and friends who spoke with him, prayed for him, and loved him. Her live experience of his humanity set her on a new course of understanding that, at the café, is activated in the exchanges between servers and guests, tour guides and visitors. Omar could not have put it better when he observed that "everyone starts smiling and it's pretty freaky." Concrete, immediate, and transformative: the Homegirl site not only constitutes an ethical commitment to the self-recognition and acceptance of the feminine, the fragmented, and the transnational circumstances of Chicana mestizaje, but also fosters the spatial actualization of this commitment, where Appalachian Whites and Irish Catholics and Puerto Rican activists can sit knee-to-knee with Omar and Aurelio, who tell us about the ways that Homeboy saved their lives.

The transformative project of consciousness raising at Homegirl Café takes place on the culinary plane as well. Called "Rosa's Mole," Zarate had been featuring mole since her days at the Plaza Café. Named for her neighbor Rosa who would watch her three children when she worked full-time at Dolores Mission, on the occasions when Rosa prepared her mole for dinner, Zarate always stayed to eat. Mole, coming from the Nahuatl *molli* (sauce; something ground), is a mixture of indigenous ingredients of Central Mexico: chiles, spices, toasted nuts and seeds, and, in red mole recipes, the bitter sweetness of Mexican chocolate.[8] Widely differing varieties are based on regional and seasonal availability, the popularity of given ingredients, and, naturally, the imaginations of home cooks and chefs who ensure that there is no end to the different flavors and styles of the thick and savory sauce.

And mole is an extremely daunting dish for the uninitiated home cook to attempt. The proportions and textures are what make mole unique to its particular creator, and the long list of ingredients, each with its own preparations, makes it one of the more intimidating kitchen experiments in the Mexican culinary catalogue. "'There are maybe a handful of people I've met in my life I would call a true genius, and Pati is one of them,' Father Greg says. When asked for proof, he offers up her mole."[9] In other words, if the Homegirl Café ethos of meeting people "where they are" can be expressed as a flavor, Zarate's mole would be it. When Zarate is asked if her recipe owes more to the Oaxacan or poblano styles, the answer is neither: "It's Los Angeles mole." The Homegirl mole, the result of a culinary legacy of colonial and indigenous hybridity, becomes newly created at the café. Instead of looking to the south in an attempt to conserve regional orthodoxies surrounding food preparation or building a culinary scaffolding around what is imagined as lost, distant, or excised, a "real" mole can come from, and tell the story of, the borderlands as a site of completion and open the palette that meets homegirls where they are. As a culinary endeavor that recuperates the homegirl identity otherwise associated with aberrant (socially deviant) behaviors and drives, Homegirl Café introduces a Chicana mestiza counterstory to the culinary marketplace that articulates the complexity of women's experiences as a source of empowerment to be embraced.

Chola vs. Chiquita Bananas and Abuelita: Alternative Mediatizations

The performative reclamation of the homegirl, or the "chola" social identity as a symbol for growing, preparing, hosting, and serving food places urban, working-class women of color at the heart of Los Angeles's culinary innovation, contributing a counternarrative that asserts a new borderlands and feminist collectivity. First, I examine the café's reclamation of the discursive power of the homegirl signifier in light of the historical objectification of the chola figure to understand how the café's repositioning signals a break from patriarchal and colonial fantasies. Next, I consider Homegirl Café's brand and values in conjunction with two dominant visual representations of "Latinas" in national food product advertising campaigns: the matronly Mexican "abuelita" and the tropical Chiquita Banana, which attempt to appeal to consumers by using Latina bodies as brand logos.

The decades of the '80s and '90s in L.A., recalled as a time that was particularly rife with gang activity, provided the context in which Norma Mendoza-Denton performed her fieldwork on the norteña/sureña (north/south) gang dynamic to learn about homegirl styles, language, and other symbolic practices. Mendoza-Denton provides the following statements that were circulated by an educational ethnographer (1) and by the president of the National District Attorney's Association (2) to consider how government authorities saw Chicana/o youths participating in homegirl signifying practices during these decades:

1. "Chola/o" refers to a Mexican-American street style that sometimes marks identification with gangs but can merely mark racial/ethnic belonging. . . . There were two groupings of cholas/os which represented two gang affiliations: sureño (south) and norteño (north). The sureños tended to be immigrant students who primarily spoke Spanish, while the norteños tended to be

second-generation Mexican-American whose primary language tool was English.

2. We know that we have come to look at stateless terrorists as our enemy and we're developing ways to stymie those attacks. And I would advance to you the theory that we are facing the same challenge and threats with the transnational gangs that are almost freely operating within our borders. In my jurisdiction, we have recently seen an increase of Hispanic or Latino gangs that are now engaging in the typical turf wars.[10]

In the first statement, youth street styles are reasoned as identity practices of "ethnic belonging." In contrast, the president of the National District Attorney Association urges readers to interpret Latino gang members as "stateless terrorists."

The institutional criminalization of working-class mestizo and Latina identity markers continued past the notorious '90s. The California Department of Justice's report *Gangs 2000* was widely distributed across police departments, schools, and teacher associations. Summarizing findings based on questions posed to criminal-justice agencies with gang units, the report states that one of the biggest contributors to the problem of street gangs was "immigrants experiencing a new culture and language difficulties."[11] In order to conduct teacher training for educators at Sor Juana High School, where Mendoza-Denton conducted her fieldwork, teachers were taught to be on the watch for immigration status, hairnets, white T-shirts, Dickies pants, and other clothing, thus providing a basis for police and teachers to detain, interrogate, and search some youths and not others. According to this logic, any of the above teen style choices or any youth "experiencing a new culture" fell into the "perp" category in the eyes government officials, educational administrators, and law enforcement officers, rendering the body of the homegirl-chola-pachuca as a target for incarceration.

If the institutional understanding of homegirls demonized her, the broader panorama of popular culture found reasons to emulate the chola's swagger. The countercultural and confrontational chola aesthetic has been copied by performing artists who want to represent toughness and hardened urban femininity. After the hip-hop generation, the homegirl look was built on meticulously coiffed hair, dark lip liner with a lighter lipstick, baggy Dickies denim or khakis, oversized flannels shirts worn open, and gold chains with Catholic iconography. Pop entertainers Gwen Stefani, Rihanna, and Selena Gomez are all famous for their interpretations, and, some have argued, misappropriations, of the homegirl aesthetic.

Moving to Chicano nationalist interpretations of homegirls, while the propensity is not to depict them as perps or terrorists, they are frequently objectified as the embodiment of dangerous erotic energies. Objectified by a patriarchal gaze through film, murals, theatre, visual art, body art, and lowrider design, she is depicted as little more than a sexual ornament on the body of a man, whose claims to "gangsta" status rest on her boundless devotion and bold eroticism, thus marginalizing the chola-homegirl potential as a borderlands subject and producer of meaning.[12] Next to Aztec gods, on the hoods of lowrider vehicles, or etched under the skin in gray-scale tattoos: the chola is cast in a supporting role, whereas the pachuco or homeboy figures at the center of the melancholic urban odyssey.

Alternatively, representations of homegirls have long appealed to Chicana writers and feminists as symbols that emphatically contest not only the patriarchal prescription of domestic confinement and self-abnegation but also the pressures to assimilate and adopt mainstream aesthetics and values. Historically, the swing-era pachucas of the 1940s broke out of prescribed gender roles and into the city's counterculture by participating in the zoot-suit fashion and lifestyle. Pachuco slang lyrics coupled with jump blues instrumentation, oversized drape-shape coats, soaring pompadour hair styles, and theatrical makeup identified war-era Mexican American women as cultural rebels during a moment of frenzied xenophobia, mass incarceration, and public rejection. Today's cholas inherit the radically confrontational self-representation of the 1940s pachucas, boldly breaking the boundaries of traditional femininity and the national mandate of cultural assimilation toward Whiteness.

Concentrating on the political implications of the pachuca-chola-homegirl figure, Rosa Linda Fregoso's excellent study examines Carmen Tafolla's 1975 early Chicano movement poem on pachuca experience.[13] In the poem's lines below, Tafolla maps the criminalization of pachucas who are viewed as "trespassers in public spaces" for their violation of the boundaries of femininity. The following excerpt relates the heightened surveillance and marginalization to which Chicana homegirls were subjected.

> So we wandered the halls
> cool chuca style
> "no se sale"
> and unawares,
> never knowing
> other junior highs were never frisked
> never knowing
> what the teachers said in the teacher's lounge
> never knowing we were (s'posed to be)
> the toughest junior high in town.[14]

Returning to the valences of the conciencia mestiza, early Chicana feminists reclaimed the homegirl figure to sound the embodied intelligence that can flow from the particular estrangement of the barrio-identified, urban, transnational woman who grapples with multiple corridors of containment and exclusion. Fregoso emphasizes the dangers of these "mujeres callejeras" (cheap, street-roaming girls) who not only fought like men but claimed the street as their domain, in frank refusal of the directive of service to family through acquiescence to domesticity and the private space of the home.

In Tey Diana Rebolledo's *Women Singing in the Snow: A Cultural Analysis of Chicana Literature* (1995), "mujeres andariegas" (women who wander and roam), the aspect of restless and unconfined women suggests women who place their individual appetites and curiosity ahead of the needs of children, husbands, and parents. But it is precisely this compulsion to defy passivity that makes homegirls (and the other machas and escandalosas Rebolledo discusses) so appropriate for feminist efforts to reorder social space: "For contemporary Chicana writers, these mujeres andariegas are quite appealing; they are women who go into male spaces such as the cantina, and appropriate them. They are the mujeres de fuerza—strong, independent women . . . in spite of the dire consequences society has predicted for them."[15] Marked by the subversion of spatial appropriateness and her defiance of the cultural paradigm of self-abnegation, the chola is read as masculine and dangerous: mean rather than maternal, she subverts

Figure 4. Inside Homegirl Café. Photo by Gregory Beylerian and Jose Zakany.

both the intracultural and national orthodoxies that seek to define and police the behavior of adolescent women.

Homeboy Industries' representation of the homegirl social identity constitutes a radical departure from the xenophobic and patriarchal conventions surrounding the chola image, while preserving the Chicana feminist reclamation of symbolic rebellion and women's empowerment. The words "homeboy" or "homegirl" appear in capital letters on the various materials and merchandise in the chunky, sans-serif NYC Regular typeface that hardens the "O" and other curved shapes into straight lines. The typography is set within a horizontal, concave rectangle, with larger letters on the sides and slightly smaller letters at the center of the rectangle. The visual impression is that of a wraparound embrace, or a bandage that curves around the homeboy and homegirl whose strength is depicted in the brick-weight lettering and the hard edges of the city. The curves embrace the hardness in an identity system that mediatizes Latinas in a way that both subverts centuries of objectification and establishes an urban, borderlands location of knowing.

In the face of the nativism described above, the Homegirl Café and the Homegirl label conveys that "home," for cholas, Latinas, and all members of the diverse cultures and ethnicities that unite under this central referent, are designated as belonging to the L.A. urban atmosphere: when they are in Los Angeles, they are *home*. But even the reclamation of home—a site of belonging and social and spatial enfranchisement—constitutes a radical gesture in a national context that marks Black and Latino bodies for exclusion and detention. Ofelia Cuevas explains that, in a nation that defines personhood through the possession of private property and venerates ownership of the single family home, Black and brown residences do not offer security from state violence.

> The residences of people of color, even when owned by their inhabitants, do not ultimately attain the status/condition of *homes*, as Radin uses the word. They are frequently and freely subject to insult and invasion by the state, often with fatal consequences for their inhabitants. As such, they cannot provide unified ethical personhood—full possession of self and future—that Radin claims for them. They are always already outside such possession, and always subject to the violence of the state.[16]

Cuevas's examination of the construction of personhood through White home ownership reveals the dark mirror lurking behind the symbolism of the "American" dream: the containment of Black and brown women and children contained in prison cells as unpaid, or close to unpaid, labor. White surplus labor could not be used in this way, as Whiteness does not become conflated with drugs, gangs, immigrants and terror in the national imaginary. Therefore, the re-vindication of "home" attached to "girl" (mestiza and Latina women and girls) contests the nativist and prison industrial matrices that mark urban Chicanas as "matter out of place" and redefines them as social actors who define local participation and write the scripts of inclusion through their specific ways of inhabiting place through style, demeanor, language, and foods. In short, homeland, for homies and homegirls, is the City of Angels, a global city characterized by transnational households and its proximity to the U.S.-Mexico border. "Patria" is not a distant place to be recalled only through tearful nostalgia: it is the neighborhoods, streets, and addresses that are defined by the homegirl.

Mainstream mediatizations of Latinidad tend to be imposed either from Spanish-language programming that attempts to construct a pan-Latino category cultural inclusion based on Latin American schema or by corporation-defined visions of how Latino-branded products are supposed to look and feel to appeal to non-Latino consumers. Univision, the most successful Spanish-language television network in the United States (whose former sports announcer Andrés Cantor was famed for his signature protracted proclamation of "Goal!" during soccer matches), has imported up to 80 percent of its programming from Latin America. According to the network's programming priorities, it defines cultural participation as the ability to recognize the latest Mexican telenovela star or the latest Miss Venezuela along with an awareness of the most recent hurricane's pathway through the Caribbean: a transnational identity that consistently looks to the Global South for the meaning and sentiments that define Latino social experience.

Unlike Univision, Homegirl Café defies the notion that Latinidad comes from across the border. As we have seen in the preceding chapters, the restaurant industry, and particularly any food that mainstream food journalism might refer to as "ethnic," tends to privilege claims of authenticity that draw on "regional" or "traditional" flavors and ingredients. The logos of Abuelita chocolate and Chiquita bananas are two of the dominant identity systems in advertising that demonstrate the market's homogenization of Latina experiences. Through the signifying power of the Mexican grandmother, Nestlé Brands perpetuates the fantasy of the classic nuclear family, with a gender-specific network of nurturance based on matronly caregiving. And through the tropicalizing trope of Chiquita bananas, colonial tensions are relieved by assurances of Latin American women's maximum desire to erotically—and agriculturally—please Anglo males.

Nestlé's Abuelita (the Spanish-language diminutive for "granny,") was commercialized in Mexico in 1939 by Fábrica de Chocolates la Azteca.[17] Packaging for the popular brand of hexagonal chocolate tablets continues to feature the face of Sara García (1895–1980), the star of Mexico's "Golden Age" of cinema. In Chicano cultural production, the preponderance of abuela representations depict her as a stalwart messenger of matronly affection flavored by "old country" customs of language, spirituality, and food. As a dominant motif in film, theatre, and literature, the playful disruption of the expectations of her caregiving nature also provide a rich source of satire, subversion, and cultural self-deprecation, as in *The George Lopez Show*'s (2002–7) sexually adventurous and narcissistic grandmother or Culture Clash's sadistic grandmother in *A Bowl of Beings* (1991), who torments her grandchild with horror stories of La Llorona at bedtime.[18] But the jurisdiction of food preparation in the Abuelita logo, and its attending ideology, is that of the matriarch of the family who is *from* (and probably *in*) Mexico, locating "authentic" food knowledge trajectories as those which flow from South to North, and from old to young. While this may not be such an upsetting paradigm (who doesn't love abuela's cooking?), it is also the expected one, and its subversion (a *chola* baking cookies?) is significant in the production of new mestiza social identities. The grandmother serves as a stand-in for an idealized Mexican past as well as for a matronly domestic realm that constitutes her axis of activity and influence.

And then we have the Chiquita Banana. Introduced in 1944, the scantily clad banana wearing a headdress made from fruit was originally voiced by Monica Lewis and drew critique for its role in perpetuating the stereotype of Latina sexual voracity. Formed in 1899, the company dominated the international banana trade and contributed to the formation of "banana republics" in Costa Rica, Honduras, and Guatemala, with deep and enduring neocolonial support of violent dictatorships to control internal development and international politics. In part to distance itself from this abusive history, in 1984 Carl Lindner Jr. spearheaded the transformation of the brand into Chiquita Brands International. In 1987 the logo also underwent an overhaul. Instead of the provocatively dressed banana, they adopted a fruit-adorned woman as their advertising logo. Capitalizing on the trope of tropicalism, in which bright colors, Afro-Cuban music, and darker (but not visibly Afro-Latino) complexions and curvaceous hips and breasts homogenize the diversity of hemispheric Latina identities and expressive cultures. According to Guzman and Valdivia,

Sexuality plays a central role in the tropicalization of Latinas through the widely circulated narratives of sexual availability, proficiency, and desirability. . . . Within the Eurocentric mind/body binary, culture is signified by the higher intellectual functions of the mind/brain while nature is signified by the lower biological functions of the body. That is, Whiteness is associated with a disembodied intellectual tradition free from the everyday desires of the body, and non-Whiteness is associated with nature and the everyday needs of the body to consume food, excrete waste, and reproduce sexually.[19]

The Chiquita banana logo saw its debut at the height of the celebrity of Hollywood's Carmen Miranda, the "Brazilian bombshell" whose bare midriff, platform shoes, and gyrating hips made her the "primary embodiment" of the United States' military and corporate priorities to seduce Latin Americans in the wake of late nineteenth-century and early twentieth-century imperialist expansionism.[20]

Agricultural reductionism of Latin America distilled into eroticism: the trope of tropicalism perpetuates, through women's bodies, the exclusive desire to please the male, Anglo gaze directed from North to South. But a very different claim to agricultural territory is made at Homegirl, not via the commonplace, feisty banana and bikini-clad vixens, but as growers. Within a year of Homegirl Café's opening at its current location on Bruno Street, Zarate had coordinated the conversion of back-alley dumpsters into raised beds for growing herbs and commandeered nearby community and local youth program plots that became teaching gardens for homegirls. As they learned the fundamentals of agriculture, they, in turn, shared their knowledge with the teens of the Dolores Mission. Now Homegirls' gardens are located at their on-site mini farm in the Homeboy Industries' parking lot, at the Dolores Mission School, at the Metabolic Studio (Los Angeles State Historic Park), and in the backyards of two members of the café's staff. All of the Homegirl gardens' produce is non-GMO and grown organically, providing 15–30 percent of the café's vegetables, herbs, citrus, wildflowers, and native plants, depending on seasonality and the success of yields.

By taking into account the central advertising campaigns of Latinas as national food logos, it is clear that Abuelita and Chiquita branding systems convey pointed ideological messages about race and gender. The visual text of the abuelita, the Mexican grandmother, stems from the propensity to mediatize Latinas as caregivers in the nuclear family unit that draws its alignment from, and remains nostalgic for, "authentic" Mexican foodways and flavors. On the other hand, the Chiquita image naturalizes neoliberal desires for an erotic, yet docile, Latina body as a guarantee of free-flowing raw materials for the U.S. Anglo male's consumption. At Homegirl Café, the image system poses a challenge to the colonial mind. Here, a transnational pachuca-chola-homegirl is vested authority by the power of her identity as an "outsider," as an enfranchised and valued participant in L.A.'s urban matrix, and as an agricultural and culinary steward who brings the embodiment of Chicana mestizaje to the public sphere.

Provider vs. Pathogen

The pages of Zarate's *Hungry for Life* (2013) cookbook, like her mole, emphasize a hybrid approach to California cuisine. Breakfast dishes like machaca (shredded beef) and eggs are offered alongside quinoa pancakes, warm faro with dried fruit, and minty chilaquiles. "Surprising combinations" could easily be the theme of Homegirl Café and its programs, as homegirls with penciled eyebrows prep and serve veggie fritters with tomato and oregano salsa or green turkey patties with chimichurri. However, *Hungry for Life* is much more than a cookbook. Like a visit to the café and Homeboy Industries' headquarters on Bruno Street, the book provides a way to meet homegirls where they are.

In between sections dedicated to recipes and exciting food presentations, Zarate shares the story of Alisha, who was arrested on the first day she held her daughter in her arms. Her daughter's twin sister had not survived. She had come to Homegirl straight out of rehab, never having cooked anything but ramen noodles up to that point. In the pages of the cookbook that combines recipes with the real stories of homegirls' lives, we see how Alisha takes on one challenge at a time and grows to become a line cook and finally one of the café's two managers. After years of sobriety, she was able to win custody of her daughter,

Elizabeth, and now helps new homegirls find their way toward self-reliance and reinvention. By providing for her daughter and training incoming participants, Alisha replaces the prison-industrial pipeline with a new kind of community based on the affirmation of the very identity markers previously associated with violence and dependency.

A glance at recent California history exposes a sharp divide between those who favor the considerable economic and social advantages of diversion programs (incarceration is proven to be far more expensive than diversion, with higher rates of recidivism),[21] and those who argue for routine criminal processing on the grounds that punishment, and not "handouts," is the moral imperative of the state. When it comes to homegirls like Alisha, the nativist narrative of Latinos portrays them as harmful intruders—with particular emphasis on the racist fears of reckless motherhood resulting in increased dependency on welfare, higher crime rates among U.S.-born children, and unchecked fertility specifically identified with the Latina woman's body. Homegirls of the Dolores Mission and East Los Angeles environments come predominantly from transnational households, to which the problems of unemployment, higher crime rates, longer welfare lines, deterioration of schools, and higher rates of teen pregnancy are attributed.

Eager to blame all social ills on the perceived influx of foreign populations, former California governor Pete Wilson's 1990s brand of nativism was rooted in nineteenth-century scientific discourses that attributed illness to the pathogenic invasion of foreign bodies.[22] Wilson's Proposition 187 moment (also known as Save Our State, or "SOS") attempted to make undocumented migrants ineligible for public social services, public health-care services (except emergency services required under federal law), and public education at elementary, secondary, and postsecondary levels. The notion that the state was "spending too much" on the welfare, education, and health services of undocumented residents fueled strategies of deportation and detention over diversion for youths in transnational households and families. Approved by California voters in 1994, the introduction to Section 1 of Proposition 187 reads:

> The People of California find and declare as follows: That
> they have suffered and are suffering economic hardship

caused by the presence of illegal immigrants in this state. That they have suffered and are suffering personal injury and damage caused by the criminal conduct of illegal immigrants in this state. That they have a right to the protection of their government from any person or persons entering this country unlawfully.[23]

If transnational families were to blame for higher crime rates, they were to be contained and neutralized, much as an infectious disease.

Late twentieth-century discourses characterizing transnational Latino families as a pressing, national criminogenic factor have not faded from view but rather have garnered new momentum with the brand of alt-right populism that put Donald Trump in the White House in 2016. One of the nation's presiding voices of the Latino-as-pathogen myth, Ann Coulter expounds on the evils of cultural diversity in her section of *Adios, America: The Left's Plan to Turn Our Country into a Third World Hellhole* (2015) titled "Immigrants: You're Not Black":

> There's no justification for civil rights laws without blacks. But under the "diversity" regime, parasites from the entire world came in and announced, *Here's a new agenda for the civil rights movement and it doesn't include you, black America....* After pretending to care about black people for approximately six minutes, Democrats ran off and redefined "civil rights" as the right to get an abortion, the right for a lesbian to take a date to her high school prom, and the right of foreigners to vote in America on ballots printed in their native language.[24]

The rampant conservatism that elected a White supremacist to the highest office in 2016 borrowed heavily from Coulter's ideology that negates any human rights–based appeals for social programs that divert, rather than detain, young people in transnational households and families, holding that they are intrinsically parasitic, even when they are citizens and eligible to vote in elections. As we see from the above invective, hostility extends to naturalized populations, who Coulter continues to call "foreigners," as well as to anyone U.S. born (think

Puerto Rico) for whom U.S. citizenship from birth and a Spanish-speaking heritage are not mutually exclusive.

If migrant members of transnational households coming from other parts of the Americas are considered pathogens and parasites, children are referred to as "monsters" and "super predators" in the nativist discussions of delinquency. In *G-Dog and the Homeboys: Father Greg Boyle and the Gangs of East Los Angeles* (2008), Father Greg details the school of thought that ultimately determines the policies and approaches to delinquency among East L.A.'s youth. "If we believe they are monsters, our public policy will reflect one thing. If we believe they are human beings, another."[25] A mind-set that communities need to parent all the children means that young people with criminal records do not get thrown away. Successful diversion programs turn to models of public health and preventative medicine to find the cause and the solution to criminogenic factors, rather than to correctional institutions and detainment, which, as Father Greg has remarked, is like trying to cure cancer by giving all the research funding to the undertakers.

A new kind of community enfranchisement was activated by the Dolores Mission when the CEBs, Father Greg, and the philanthropist Ray Stark united in the shared vision of reclaiming the youth as their own, and as community members "our sons and daughters," intrinsically worthy of love and compassion just as they were. Rather than envision "success" stories, Father Greg's ministry takes inspiration from the words of Mother Theresa, who says, "We are not called to be successful, but faithful."

The transversion endorsed and performed by Homegirl Café supplants the pathogen myth with that of the provider and, recalling Sandoval, creates a social movement on a site that had been once overlooked because it was "perceived as limited, restricted by gender, sex, or race identity." This reclamation of what twentieth-century nativists have feared, rejected, and punished has witnessed a discernable role reversal in the way it has expanded out from the Homegirl Café and is now celebrated by the city's administration on many fronts. Los Angeles now claims homies as its very own, evinced by LAX Airport and city hall locations that are provisioned by Homegirl Café under the Homeboy Industries label.

The post-9/11 airport dining industry has adapted to cater to clients facing increased wait times and seen a bourgeoning national consumer demand for locally sourced and fresh ingredients to take the place of the ultraprocessed and unhealthy offerings at fast-food chains that were the stalwart of airport dining in recent decades past. Moreover, an increased desire for a sense of "place" has influenced airport culinary culture, so that successful hospitality groups today, rather than exclusively drawing in national licensed and franchised restaurant brands for their terminals, are rethinking what the terminal allows the city to say about itself and emphasizing how local chefs best represent a city's culinary activity.[26] To give travelers a true sense of place, airports are seeking a highly differentiated product—not just a meal to get through and a terminal to get past, but an opportunity to savor what is relevant and representative of the region. As such, the significance of Homeboy food products in the LAX terminal cannot be overstated. Debuting in 2013, all purchases of grab-and-go, Latin-influenced salads, sandwiches, pastries, and wraps as well as apparel and other merchandise with the Homeboy and Homegirl logos benefit Homeboy's programs.[27] Rather than making headlines as the youth population that the city needs to protect itself against, the Homeboy presence in the airport terminal redesignates what was considered parasitic and celebrates homie and homegirl contributions, not only as food workers but as the story the city wants to tell about itself on an international level. The homies and their products now are kin both to the CEBs of the Dolores Mission as well as to an entire city that articulates through its airport terminal how Homeboy Industries represents what is best about itself.

After the recession, Father Greg and Homeboy Industries were hit hard by falling donations and the difficulties of job placement for homies completing their training programs. Homeboy found an unusual ally in Bruce Karatz, the multimillionaire and former chief executive of KB Home, who was facing felony charges related to the manipulation of executive stock options. In search of his own second chance, Karatz volunteered to help Homeboy climb out of a $5 million deficit and apply his skills and connections toward a higher purpose. By helping to broker a deal with Ralphs grocery stores to sell Homeboy chips and salsa and urging Father Greg to apply for the unoccupied café space on the second floor of city hall, Karatz was instrumental in increasing revenue at a precarious time for philanthropic endeavors,[28] and they celebrated their grand opening of Homeboy Diner in June 2011 in city hall.

Perhaps the apex of the role reversal from pathogen to provider finds its culminating message in a June 2011 headline of *Los Angeles Downtown News* that reads: "Homeboys Feeding City Hall."[29] As providers, the youth that had been previously targeted as pathogens and predators are now positioned as "feeders." Before Homeboy Diner opened, "City Hall had been a virtual food desert. There were snack machines in the basement and some council offices kept candy bowls, but for anything more substantial, staffers were forced to leave the building."[30] In the above press coverage of the Homeboy Diner's opening, the city hall edifice is characterized in terms of lack and want. Now, homeboys and homegirls are viewed as what the city needs in order to thrive, from its public officials to the airport terminal patrons who increasingly want restaurants that not only provide meals but make a declarative statement about who they are as part of a global metropolis.

So far I have discussed the potential of Homegirl Café and its associated image system to counter the patriarchal and neoliberal mediatizations of Latinas in the culinary marketplace, but it's equally important to understand whether or not Homegirl Café's mediatization of young, at-risk Angelina women truly constitutes an alternative visual paradigm without also resorting to objectification. With homies and homegirls providing food services in the symbolically significant spaces of city hall and LAX, we need to ask: What pacts have been made that, once again, trade on mestiza bodies to fulfill the desires of spectators that come from more privileged socioeconomic circumstances than the women depicted in the cookbook or referenced on the T-shirt's logo? To answer this question, it's helpful to look at two scenarios that swerve noticeably into object-making rather than subject-making imaginaries, specifically Ana Puga's examination of the conventions of fictional melodrama and Saidiya V. Hartman's investigation of White pleasure in the face of the spectacle of enslaved bodies in the nineteenth century. In Puga's study, the tropes of theatrical melodrama are deployed to frame suffering as an individual journey, while obscuring the political economy of suffering:

In this economy, suffering is not just passively endured; it is actively traded. Both migrants and authors/directors who view themselves as empathic with migrants participate in a variety of transactions in which suffering functions sometimes as commodity and sometimes as currency. Suffering-as-commodity may be packaged and sold with the help of authors, publishers, directors, and film producers. Suffering-as-currency is traded for empathy, sympathy, or solidarity that may in turn facilitate mobility.[31]

If homies are subsumed by the suffering-as-commodity and suffering-as-currency paradigms, then is Homegirl Café championing Latina womanhood by reproducing a formulation of subaltern suffering as that which is written onto the individual and overcome only through a series of personal decisions? Or worse, are the Chiquita Banana and Abuelita being replaced by what Hartman has called the "hyperembodiness of the powerless," offering the mestiza body up for inspection and reinforcing its "thingness," this time not for the tropicalist Chiquita trope or the myth of matronly domesticity, but for its excess of pain as a "sentimental resource and/or locus of enjoyment"?[32] In the conventions of theatrical melodrama interrogated by Puga, as with the stagings of the suffering Black body theorized by Hartman, pain is the currency that purchases empathy, but this means that brokenness, rather than embodied imaginaries of transformation and rebellion, is the discursive focus.

Here, Father Greg's evocation of Mother Theresa's understanding of faith ("we are not called to be successful, but faithful") provides an insight about Homeboy Industries' objectives that helps us interpret the subject-making potential of their image systems. The writings of both Zarate and Boyle include the stories of young men and women that have not managed to complete their training and recovery programs, yet these youth remain part of how Zarate and Boyle refer to and define their community, reminding audiences and observers that at-risk and formerly incarcerated youths are not to be construed as lone individuals up against poverty-as-a-force-of-nature, but rather their fate is the community's expression of its moral responsibility as an article of faith. The Boyle Heights neighborhood, through the work of the Dolores Mission and Homeboy Industries, resolved to care for its own. Not the suffering Other, but the imperfect self: the homeboys and homegirls are portrayed with their defiance intact, and individual "successes" and "failures" do not determine a homie's value to the community: they are no less than the mirror image of the community itself.

Homegirl Café as Culinary Counterstory

Omar was about to wrap up our visit on the second floor of Homeboy Industries where administrative activities and classroom instruction takes place. In what felt a little like asking for an encore performance, I asked if he could tell us more about the life experiences that led him to seek out Father Greg and Homeboy services. He and Aurelio generously conducted us into a small, empty conference room with a window that looked out onto the large, professional bakery where homies and homegirls clad in white were focused on their tasks. I saw a young woman in street clothes enter the premises and approach a large man in his baker's uniform. Walking slowly, performing a clear "don't mess with me" message in her gait and demeanor, she suddenly dropped the 'tude and lunged at the man with what was easily the world's most ecstatic embrace. This fierce zeal was enthusiastically returned by the burly recipient of her hug. Directing my attention back to the room, we sat ourselves at the conference table opposite Omar and his trainee Aurelio, who had been quiet throughout the entire visit. Taking a risk, I asked if he wouldn't mind sharing something of his own circumstances that brought him into Homeboy's fold. He agreed.

"I'm here because I had a bad day. I woke up, and knew I was going to kill someone."

When Aurelio spoke, I stopped taking notes. His words were so unadorned and raw that you could feel an ionic shift in the room. That day went differently for Aurelio than what he had planned and did not result in a homicide or a conviction, but the close calls drew him out and onto a different path. Hearing him speak honestly of his choices created the possibility of empathy, as we were there together witnessing how the brutality Aurelio grew up in had not been his invention but what had been thrust on him from birth.

We learned that one of Aurelio's significant challenges was to simply get a haircut. His barber shop sat behind enemy lines, and even though he was no longer a member of a gang, his appearance there would bring out rivals to challenge and threaten him. Getting a quick trim could mean losing his life. Aurelio turned this hard reflection into a joking apology for his hairstyle. We laughed with him—a cholo used to associating with felons apologizing for his 'do. But the sincere glee that we shared at that moment didn't come from Aurelio's self-deprecating humor—it came from our admiration for his strength.

Taking into account the majoritarian stories that dominate national conversations about the presence of transnational Latino families, increasingly criminalized Latinx citizens and denizens in the second decade of the millennium, and the mediatized tropes that alternate between the hypersexualization of Latinas and their confinement to roles of enclosed domesticity, Homegirl Café's conviction (beginning at the Dolores Mission in 1988) to meet homies and homegirls where they are provides a new site for the liberatory project of la conciencia mestiza to thrive. In the Homegirl Café and Homeboy Industries environment, the hierarchies of reformer/reformed are neutralized by creating a space in which homies are the teachers, hosts, growers, creators, servers, and stewards of a contextual knowledge of recovery to create what Anzaldúa describes as a "new story to explain the world and our participation in it, a new value system with images and symbols that connect us to each other and to the planet."[33] With the literal "amasamiento," the act of kneading and forming dough in the hands of youths united under the Homegirl signifier, one can discern the full ideation of a new mestiza counterstory reshaping the public imaginary in the culinary marketplace.

Chapter 4

FROM JUAN VALDEZ TO THIRD WAVE CAFÉS

Lattes and Latinidad in the Marketplace

The Bean Scene

I've always loved the coffeehouse.[1] As a teenager exploring the bitter shock of my first espresso in Pasadena, to the open mics where I shared my adolescent poetic compositions amid the sounds of the cappuccino machine and the aroma of the evening's brew, from high school to college and well beyond, coffeehouses have been central to my flow of words and ideas and have paved the way toward productivity with the singular seduction of a strong cup and the mild distractions of an atmosphere away from the austerity of the office or the commotion of home. I wrote much of *Women and Knowledge in Mesoamerica* (2011) in the café area of the bygone Borders bookstore in Oak Park, Illinois, where I would ply my son Emiliano with the comics section and hot chocolate in exchange for an hour or two of dedicated writing time.

Along with my routine visits to coffeehouses came the frequent exposure to portrayals of humble mestizo and indigenous agricultural workers in places such as Mexico and Guatemala. Ostensibly there to provide a visual reassurance of the business's commitment to "ethical sourcing" and "fair trade" relationships, I wanted to provide a critical reading of this imaging system to situate these portraits of mestizaje and indigeneity within a context of the U.S. mediatization of Latinx cultures in advertising. It was always clear, as I stood in line for coffee or visited a restroom decorated by photographs of a Guatemalan festival, that the people in the photos were not the same ones buying high-end coffee from these boutique cafés. And, as a Latina coffee enthusiast (not to say addict), I wanted to examine the ways that the images created mestizo public identities, given the historical, hemispheric linkage between Latin American bodies and agricultural essentialism.

My ensuing analysis sustains Arelene Dávila's premise that "the reconstruction of individuals into consumers and populations into markets are central fields of cultural production that reverberate within public understanding of people's place, and hence of their rights and entitlements, in a given society."[2] As high-end coffee culture has grown into an all-pervading feature of the metropolis, its commercial representations of Latinos and Latin Americans inform attitudes about which bodies belong where in the continuum of the production and consumption of coffee.

While most sources of caffeine are consumed where they grow (more tea is consumed in India and China than anywhere else, and these places rank first and second in its global production), coffee and cacao (chocolate) break from this pattern, with consuming nations located far from their source.[3] Beginning in the tenth century, nomadic peoples of Ethiopia ate the plant's red cherries, and Sufi pilgrims of Islam spread the beverage throughout the Middle East. In the early part of the seventeenth century, Venetian merchants brought the first sacks of coffee to western Europe, where its fragrance and stimulating effects led to the rapid emergence of coffeehouses throughout Europe. After Dutch and English vessels exported the plant to the Americas, the regions of Brazil, Central America, and the tropical parts of South America came to dominate the global tree cultivation and production by the early twentieth century.

In the borderlands vernacular, "pinto" and "jumping" might be the beans most commonly associated with mestizo identities, but the coffee bean, picked in the Western Hemisphere by Latin American hands, constitutes the second-most traded commodity on the planet after crude oil. This section defines the key referents needed to enter the conversation about lattés, third wave coffee, and mestizo imagery in the marketplace. The next section will provide an overview of the famous Juan Valdez figure, which was central to paving the way for second wave coffee consumption in the United States, while conserving a very different meaning in Colombia, the place of Juan Valdez's national origin. The ensuing section investigates the concepts of "fair washing" and "noblesse oblige" and their significance in the construals of ethical commitments made by Blue Bottle Coffee and Starbucks, two third wave coffee companies most representative of the high-end coffee industry's relationship to fair trade. At the chapter's conclusion,

I interrogate the repeated occurrence of brown bodies in the marketing of coffee products to understand how mestizo and Latino public identities are shaped by these image systems and the ideologies that they sustain.

The United States imports the second-largest amount of coffee beans in the world, with its top three suppliers including Brazil, Colombia, and Vietnam.[4] According to the National Coffee Association, out-of-home coffee consumption reached an all-time high of 46 percent in 2017.[5] Some thirty years after Starbucks opened its original store in Seattle in 1971, the Starbucks Corporation introduced ethical coffee-sourcing guidelines developed in partnership with Conservation International, placing its growth as a leader in ethical retail practices as a priority of its brand that not only has provided customers with one of the highest price tags for a cup of coffee but has cornered the market on the development of the millennial "coffee culture," emphasizing sleek, metropolitan atmospheres for youthful urbanites. As of 2017, the number of Starbucks stores worldwide was 27,339. For scale, the number of McDonald's worldwide for the same year was 36,899.[6]

The descriptor "third wave" came into usage to articulate the shift taking place in the national consumption of coffee from a commodity to an artisanal product comparable to fine wine. Coffee expert Timothy J. Castle discussed the recent history of coffee consumption in terms of "waves" in December 1999, proposing that the first was characterized early on by the purchase of coffee as a raw ingredient to be roasted at home to the ubiquitous preground product sold in cans (late 1800s–1960s). Trish Skeie from Taylor Maid Farms Organic Coffee and Tea also discusses the first wave as the national proliferation of canned coffee, when the beverage was to be consumed, but not necessarily savored. Advertisements featured ecstatic housewives enjoying the luxury of "good to the last drop" instant coffee, and diners and doughnut shops were the main public destinations for social coffee consumption. The first wave witnessed its terminal years from 1960 to 1988, when domestic coffee consumption dropped from 74 percent of the population to 50 percent.[7]

The second wave came about as a reaction to the lack of freshness and quality that was pervasive in U.S. coffee products in the 1980s. The need for a coffee market overhaul was then met by "specialty" beverages geared toward more sophisticated consumers. The second wave saw the introduction of flavored espresso beverages, the abandonment of the cheap robusta coffee bean in favor of the more flavorful arabica variety, and the proliferation of coffee shops as a destination for the young and affluent.[8] And it was this second wave that witnessed the deployment of Latinidad to direct the gaze from consumers in the Global North to producers in the Global South. Thanks to the vision of the Doyle Dane Bernbach ad agency, the Valdez advertisements featured their protagonist sharing details about his coffee harvest, such as the ways in which soil, bean varietals, and altitude make a critical difference in the beverage's taste. Starbucks and Peets followed in this vision as Valdez's second wave drew attention to the benefits of specific types of beans and harvesting methods.

In spite of the recent development by which the "latte," an Italian-origin coffee drink made with espresso and steamed milk, has come to be synonymous with "snobbery" by Republican Party propagandists, any serious third wave coffee drinker would not deign to touch the stuff. The third wave constituted a new devotion to sourcing and roasting techniques—a refinement that was more about letting the coffee bean "speak for itself" rather than the wash of syrups and frothy dairy (and dairy alternatives) diluting the pure flavors of the highest quality beans and roasting techniques.[9] Now, third wave coffee vendors focus on special-origin beans, roasting styles, importation, and detailed narratives about the company's relations with growers in the developing world. Images of Latin American coffee workers and growers are strategically placed to bolster consumer confidence in labels such as "shade grown," "fair trade," and "direct trade."

With the first wave, the dominant corporations (Nestlé, General Foods, Philip Morris) had sought to increase profits by providing cheaper, less flavorful beverages to be consumed frugally at home. With Starbucks leading the charge by monopolizing the "third place" (neither home nor work) strategy with luxurious atmospherics and specialized products, the advent of cyber society also fueled the demand for spaces that permitted both social and solitary endeavors. Third wave companies focus on whole bean sales in one pound bags, promote in-store consumption of brewed drip coffee and an array of espresso beverages, and, significantly, provide an abundance of electrical outlets for the Wi-Fi set.

For brands like Starbucks that rely on the "third space" strategy, interior design is central to their allure, and portraits of coffee harvesters feature prominently in their dining areas as a central advertising trope that acts like décor. The word "advertise" means, in its simplest denotation, to inform, to notify. Advertising, in its commercial context as the visual and audial dimensions of a given product's marketing campaign, constitutes a paid message from an identifiable source created and positioned for the purpose of persuasion. The symbols, language, and other attending audial and visual information, are designed to capture the attention and desires of a certain group of people—not as a totalizing project that presumes to mean only one thing to all comers but for a select and intentional audience that is defined ahead of time by participants in the advertising process. Potential consumers then create meaning out of the information, reasoning, and emphasis delivered through the ad's claims. A relationship between sponsor, advertising professionals, and consumers constitutes the cycle of advertising messages and their reach.[10] Examining commercial representations as constitutive of cultural identities, ads do not just tell you what to buy, they tell you who you are.

The last establishing term of the chapter I define here is Latinidad, which I employ as it is used by Beltrán, who explains it as a "sociohistorical process whereby various Latin American national-origin groups are understood as sharing a sense of collective identity and cultural consciousness."[11] At its most contradictory, the notion of Latinidad supposes a collective Latino identity in the face of diverse experiences relating to immigration, race, gender, class, religion, language, and other issues. At its most useful, and in spite of its homogenizing implications, Latinidad provides a descriptor for the pan-Latino experience of institutional racism, stereotyping, and shared cultural knowledge of hemispheric domination by the United States. My use of Latinidad here seeks to call attention to the ways that Latinx audiences are impacted by a discrete set of political vulnerabilities that are silenced and effaced by the performativity of coffee in second and third wave marketing campaigns. While the terms mestizo, Latinx, and Latino are employed throughout my study, here, the terms "Hispanic" and "Latin" make an appearance, as these are the census- and marketing-sanctioned designations used most frequently in the business and government sources I discuss.

Juan Valdez and the Fetish of the Agricultural Other

Latinos occupy a middle ground in terms of their representation in advertising. They appear in ads less frequently than blacks but more often than Asian-Americans and American Indians. Historically, they have been pictured in mainstream advertising hosting dinner parties, washing dishes or drinking coffee.

ADAGE, "MINORITIES: REPRESENTATIONS IN ADVERTISING"

In the United States, Latinos and references to Latinidad populate the world of advertising on various fronts. As creative professionals among the top ranks of the advertising industry, as target audiences for companies aiming to expand into the Hispanic market, and, more grimly, as caricatured representations intended to target non-Latino consumers, the scope of national campaigns reflects varied levels of engagement with Latino identity formation in marketing campaigns. This section deals with advertising's deployment of neocolonial portrayals of Latino culture, with a specific focus on the history and interpretation of the Juan Valdez figure as a multivalent representative of the power dynamic between the coffee consuming North and the coffee-producing South.

First, it's useful to know how all three areas of advertising combine to create the broader field of image systems that are varyingly created by, for, or in spite of Hispanic advertising professionals and potential consumers. Although they continue to be underrepresented in the professional world of advertising, Latinos have contributed significantly to national campaigns for mainstream audiences.[12] According to the Bureau of Labor Statistics, of the 582,000 Americans employed in advertising and communications in 2014, less than half were women, 6.6 percent were Black or African American, 5.7 percent identified as Asian, and 10.5 percent were "Hispanic."[13] Considering that the Census Bureau reported that Latinos make up 17.6 percent of the nation's residents, with a population of 56.6 million in 2015,[14] and that, in 2015, Latinos controlled $1.3 trillion in buying power, it would stand to reason that companies and advertising executives in the business of expanding their markets would be encouraging greater inclusivity of peoples of Latin American descent.[15]

Although people of color have yet to attain parity in the field of advertising, Latinos are not new to the world of professional marketing in the United States. Working across cultural and language differences with clients in the 1960s and 1970s, when industry executives began to court minority business through focused marketing campaigns, Latina women, in particular, held salient positions as owners of advertising firms and provided award-winning work for companies such as Ford and Pepsi.[16] However, many of the mainstream campaigns for multinational clients did not refer to Latinidad in overt ways, so the public would have had little or no knowledge of the scope of Hispanic participation in the marketing campaigns designed by Latino innovators in the advertising world.

By the early 1990s, ethnic/multicultural marketing became the mantra of contemporary promotion plans. This new marketing paradigm views the market as "divided into segments and aims at gathering information regarding the customers, traditions, rituals, relationships and identities of these segments of potential consumers."[17] Marketers realized that media that successfully appealed to diverse audiences with culturally relevant messages would have the greatest chance for success, but this compartmentalization of consumer courtship led to very different branding and imaging strategies, thereby reproducing and normalizing hierarchies based on race and class to which the sponsors and ad agencies subscribed.

Practices targeting the consumer power of Latino populations were rooted in the inception of U.S. Spanish-language media, which, by the end of the 1950s, remained limited to the local level. When Televisa, the Mexican television giant, purchased entire Spanish-language stations in San Antonio and Los Angeles, rather than carving out programming on English-language stations, it provided the dominant concepts in Latino marketing, such as the assumption that the Hispanic market existed only in the Spanish language, only on a segregated channel, and followed a totally separate trajectory from the mainstream market.[18] The presumed "foreignness" of Latinos in the United States continues to be a trope that emphasizes the distance between Latin America and the Global North and belies the demographic realities of English-dominant Latinos who may never tune in to programming on Spanish-language networks.

Marketing has played a part in concretizing many commonly held stereotypes about Latinos. Collective orientation, articulated by an emphasis on strong family ties and a lack of individual drives and motivations, is perhaps the most prevalent message delivered by Latino advertising. Ads also play up the dichotomies between Anglo and Latino cultures, either showing that Latinos are superior to Anglos in exciting ways (a Budweiser commercial shows the superiority of Latino masculinity because Latino men can handle the spice from habanero peppers, while their otherwise tough gringo counterparts cannot) or by foregrounding Latino astonishment at finally having access to products associated with the developed world by using descriptors such as "new," "fast," and "modern." Cultural pride is signified by sombreros and maracas, or an unambiguous "Latin" look that any casting director understands to mean dark, straight hair and an olive complexion with features that owe more to Mediterranean appearances than to the Afro-Latino or indigenous ancestries that define large swaths of the Latin American population.[19]

If these are the depictions that are intended to entice Latino viewing publics, there are also a range of ads that are clearly launched at the expense of Latino brand loyalty. In the previous chapters, I have set forth illustrations of these figures that loom large in the popular imagination. The Chiquita Banana character began in 1944, with Chiquita stickers on each banana starting in 1947, making it nearly impossible to have breakfast without evoking the Carmen Miranda–inspired stereotype of the hypersexual Latina clown. And then there was Frito Bandito, developed by Frito Lay in the 1960s, against whom the Mexican-American Anti-Defamation Committee filed suit. And let's not forget the delights of the Taco Bell Chihuahua from 1997 to 2000, which led to a national storm of utterances in the Chihuahua's mock Spanish accent and, like the bandito, was phased out owing to the efforts of Hispanic advocacy groups.[20]

As Ramirez Berg points out, our constant categorization of the diverse figures and forms that comprehend the matrix of human activity in our surroundings stems from the primordial need for self-preservation and safety. Our mind needs to file information about how to predict dangers and threats: a basic skill that enables our survival. However, this same propensity that keeps us safe can have harmful consequences when category-making meets with ethnocentrism and prejudice. In mass media, category-making is not value neutral, and the Chiquita Banana, Frito Bandito, and Taco Bell Chihuahua images so pervasive in U.S. households generate values that preserve and naturalize North American dominance over a Latin American Other that is invariably imperfect and incomplete.[21]

The advertising world is also slow to distance African American images from a colonial past. As Marilyn Kern-Foxworth points out, Black stereotypes in advertising reveal a particular pattern in food-product promotion:

> It was difficult to prepare a meal without using food products featuring a stereotypical pickaninny, black mammy, or black Sambo. In other words, the use of blacks in pejorative and stereotypical advertising kept them emotionally bound to the idiosyncratic whims of their former masters. With advertising, former slave owners became masters over different objects. They made them subservient. They made them docile. They made them act stupid. They made them appear ignorant. They made them ugly. They made them grotesque. They made them want to be white. These symbols not only continued but proliferated around the turn of the century with the overwhelming success of Uncle Ben, The Gold Dust Twins, Rastus and Aunt Jemima.[22]

More than a century and a half after the abolition of slavery, consumers can still "own" Blacks as objects in their homes. Emotionally bound to their households in subservient roles, these ignorant, docile, and unattractive figures make routine appearances on the typical U.S. breakfast table.

Which brings us to the riddle of Juan Valdez. Beginning with his 1959 birth year, the series of television ads popular from the early '60s to the late '80s depicting the iconic farmer with his serape, moustache, and mule, Conchita, set the stage on which Latin American bodies are placed to stimulate coffee consumption in the United States. In the scope of advertising, he's viewed as one of the best pitchmen in modern times. According to a 2001 *New York Times* article, "Awareness of Juan Valdez in the United States stood at 60 percent last year, with logo identification of Café de Colombia reaching 85 percent, ahead of Nike and Michelin," and first-year marketing students at Harvard University study Juan Valdez, not only because of the phenomenon of his advertising success but also because of the tangible contributions his campaign brought Colombia's economy.[23] With Juan Valdez's meteoric ascension as an internationally known figure, can we place him on the same level of the breakfast table's racial stereotypes that inspire self-hatred rather than self-recognition across Latino viewing publics? The answer to this question is not straightforward but wholly complex, hemispheric, and contextual.

When I look at the ways that advertisements appeal to potential consumers, my litmus test for neocolonial framing is whether the image invokes self-recognition or represents a depiction of the Other in service to members of the Western elite. In my search for the truth about Juan Valdez, an unexpected conversation with a graduate student and collaborator proved helpful. When I told John Cruz, who was then a PhD candidate in my department with expertise in Latin American film and marketing, about the theme of my chapter, he went silent and his eyes turned into wide, sparkling circles filled with surprise, affection, and excitement. According to Cruz, it's really a very simple algorithm: Juan Valdez is Colombia. Colombia is Juan Valdez.

Cruz's algorithm is substantiated in the pages of *Federación Nacional de Cafeteros de Colombia, 1927–2017* (2017). The fifty-year celebration of Juan Valdez's legacy as a fictive Colombian persona and brand representative was celebrated in 2010, where he has long served as the symbol of the superiority of the Colombian product, as well as the identity of its people.[24] Juan Valdez and his mule Conchita symbolize the country's nobility, prosperity, and future prospects (similar to how the United States regards its Statue of Liberty) by spreading the message of Colombian coffee throughout the world.

> No existe prácticamente ningún aspecto de la vida colombiana que no esté íntimamente ligado al café: el transporte, la salud, la educación, la investigación, la re-creación y todas las expresiones de la cultura tienen estrechos vínculos con esos símbolos que representan a Colombia en el mundo: Juan Valdez, su mula *conchita* y la imponente cordillera de los Andes como fondo.[25]

Juan Valdez represents the agricultural worker in Colombia, in each aspect of his figure and form. His sombrero, carriel (leather satchel), poncho, apron, espadrilles, and mule all tell the story of the Paisa countryside in the state (department) of Antioquia. It is a proud but unquestionably difficult life. No tractor or heavy machinery can perform the labor for Valdez: it's up to him and Conchita to carry the coffee down the mountainside to where the muleteers gather to sell the hard-won fruits of their labor.

Throughout our conversation, Cruz excitedly shows me photos of Colombian chapoleras, the women whose hands pick the coffee. Hailing from the Antioquean region, his own aunt had been a chapolera, and he grew up visiting the fields with his aunts and uncles as a child. "In Colombia, Juan Valdez is our pride." On December 12, 2002, the first Juan Valdez Café store opened its doors at El Dorado International Airport in Bogotá. "When Starbucks came to Colombia," explains Cruz, "we asked ourselves, how can this be possible? Colombians have to support their own brand. Going to Starbucks would be like taking out a knife and stabbing myself."

In Cruz's closet hangs a Juan Valdez costume that he has donned for Halloween in Columbus, Ohio. "Everyone knew who I was," he tells me. "I was surprised. So many Americans know Juan Valdez." He let me know that any self-respecting Colombian who travels away from their country takes coffee as a gift for friends and hosts. Avoiding Starbucks back home and giving Juan Valdez his business, he recognizes that the two chains serve very different purposes. Cruz explains that at Juan Valdez, customers have their coffee with a newspaper or they gather with family or friends. It's not the type of environment that is conducive to an open laptop and focused work. "Besides, someone would snatch up the laptop and it would be gone," notes Cruz.[26]

That Valdez is a folk hero whose star power could only be compared to that of the pop star Shakira is emphasized in Laura Kiniry's article for the *Smithsonian* (2011):

> "There's very little difference between Juan Valdez and Elvis, as both have transcended coffee and music to become cultural icons of their respective countries," says Doug Towne, editor at the Society of Commercial Archeology (SCA), an organization that helps preserve, document and celebrate the 20th-century commercial landscape. But Valdez is dissimilar to say, the Jolly Green

Giant or the Cracker Jack Sailor. More than a marketing tool, he represents a very real and vital percentage of Colombian society. "Juan Valdez has become the embodiment of Colombia," says Towne. "Kind of like if the American flag, baseball and apple pie could be personified in a single U.S. citizen."[27]

Café de Colombia ®

Figure 5. Juan Valdez Café de Colombia logo.

Juan Valdez as a domestic brand and a national culture meets Juan Valdez as a global enterprise. From the first café in 2002, establishments are now found in the United States, Chile, Ecuador, Aruba, Panama, Bolivia, Costa Rica, El Salvador, Mexico, and Paraguay. Packaged coffee is also sold in Europe and Asia, and online sales are offered in China, the United States, and Germany.[28] However, in spite of the Colombian pride in the national tradition of superior coffee, Cruz acknowledges that the best beans are selected and reserved exclusively for export. Like unstinting hosts, the best is only for guests. This small fact says a lot about Colombian self-recognition as producers, rather than consumers, of Juan Valdez's most prized achievement.

While in the Colombian context this figure is a beloved representation reflecting the reality of many rural workers, in the North, Juan Valdez creates a different kind of public identity that provides a major genealogical moment in the linkage between Latinidad and coffee consumption. In the U.S. setting, a view of Juan Valdez located in the South, wearing his traditional garb and bursting with agricultural felicity, implies the dominant nation's consumption of Latin

American raw materials, and the specter of Latin American bodies performing arduous manual labor are packaged and publicized as the ancestral—even spiritual—directive of workers who take delight in their unchanging and picturesque poverty.

When the New York agency Doyle Dane Bernbach saw the marketing potential in the Juan Valdez figure to serve as an ambassador for Colombian coffee, they tapped into a very real aspect of Colombian heritage with which many sectors of Colombian society would both identify and embrace. As the third-largest coffee-producing country in the world, in 2009 Colombia produced 8.1 million 132-pound sacks of coffee. Approximately 30 percent of all rural areas depend on the coffee crop for economic survival, and 95 percent are small producers running family operations that sell exclusively to the National Federation of Coffee Growers of Colombia, creators of Juan Valdez.[29] However, an understanding of modernization theory helps to understand how, in a U.S. context, the Juan Valdez figure is tied to a history of colonial economic domination. Proponents of modernization theory, the most prevalent school of thought regarding poverty and development in the Third World, maintain a view of these societies as being largely "traditional." Western Europe and the United States, according to this logic, have left the traditional era to move into modern economic growth as the cultural norm. The traditional society, then, is defined by its stagnation and continuity of the emotional ties to ancestors through the performance of traditional duties and ritual, which represents the pathway to honor. In this framework, there is no emphasis on accumulation, personal wealth, or economic development. Adherents to the promise of modernization theory hold that capitalism, and its incentivization of competition, growth, and political and economic departure from ancestral values, will effectively "rescue" Third Worlders from the poverty and backwardness that moors them to failure. Measuring societal evolution according to stages of economic advancement, this view understands that the United States and Western Europe have achieved economic maturity, as evinced by their participation in wealthy standards of living and high-speed consumption.[30]

The dependency school, on the other hand, does not see poor countries as primitive, unchanged states. Neither traditional, nor accidental, dependency theory sees the impoverishment of the Third

World as a requirement for the expansion of the industrial. Producing raw materials and vulnerable to predatory legal structures, capitalist domination depends on low-wage occupations to produce goods for export. In the area of agriculture, workers are violently forced *out* of traditional economic structures and heritage agricultural practices in order to perform cash crop labor to supply rubber, cotton, sugar, tobacco, and coffee for export. Following Aidan Foster-Carter's understanding of "underdevelopment" as a transitive verb, dependency theory may best be summarized by thinking of the connection between dominant and subordinate nations as "I underdevelop you."[31]

Returning to the question about whether our Juan Valdez does or does not constitute the perpetuation of a colonial stereotype, our answer must come from an understanding of modernization and dependency. For the Colombian nationals that Cruz discusses, the icon is an intimate, folkloric iteration of relatable rural experience. Perhaps like a cowboy in representations of the U.S. Southwest or a steelworker in the northern Midwest states, the chapoleras in their full skirts and tall, wide-brimmed hats and the muleteers with their faithful beasts all shared in the cultivation of coffee to which the nation's economic prospects and cultural life were inextricably bound. For over half a century, Juan Valdez has represented the dignity and hopes of half a million cafeteros (coffee farmers) who harvest their beans within Colombia.

In contrast, nostalgia for colonial relationships tint the coffee market's references to symbolic Latin Americanness in mainstream campaigns. Linda C. L. Fu analyzes commercial branding and coloniality in contemporary advertisements for companies such as Louis Vuitton (1984), in which two Asian men in "coolie" attire and pigtails transport a luxurious leather bag on a litter, and a Southward White Beer (2007) ad in which dark-skinned "native" people perform acts of torture on horrified Whites. "In terms of the themes in which imageries of the racial Other are utilized, traditional ones (with the exception of slavery ads), such as the appropriation and commodification of a quasi-logical racial hierarchy and the range of racialized metaphors and depictions that have a long history of exploiting imageries of the racial Other, not only continue to exist but have also, in a sense, been renewed and remodeled within both public interest and commercial campaigns."[32] In the national context, Juan Valdez represents Latin

American gratitude for the Northern economic framework of modernization, and sells, along with the "perfect cup," the redemptive aspects attributed to capitalism and consumption. Juan Valdez naturalizes the notion that White consumers bring happiness and fulfillment to the agricultural Other, who wants nothing to do with the complications of high-speed commerce and the accumulation of capital. Not a self-portrait for consumers in the North, instead Juan Valdez becomes the representation of the producing Other, who is ever cast in terms of his fidelity to the "ancestral" joy of plantation work.

Blue Bottle and Starbucks: Fair Washing and Noblesse Oblige

In marketing third wave coffee with photographic portraits of Latin American and African peoples, the customer's attention is strategically directed to the visual index of a Third World Other that is frozen in time in an agricultural pursuit. The representation of rural workers, in turn, both expiates and encourages high-end coffee purchases by articulating a connection between consumer and worker, denoting the workers' simultaneous poverty and gratitude in relation to the consuming urban class. The images in third wave coffee shops may not, as stand-alone visual artifacts, constitute colonial messages of racial supremacy and subjugation. An aesthetic judgment, separate from the visual context of marketing campaigns for high-end cafés, would facilitate an entirely different set of interpretations. Taken merely as art photography, the print below featured on the Starbucks website to illustrate their One Tree for Every Bag Commitment campaign in Chiapas, Mexico, may be described in terms of its foreground and background, frame, perspective, use of positive and negative space, and the relationship between the major figure and the background, among other formal elements present in the image. However, the photograph does not exist in a vacuum but is, instead, inextricably moored to the tensions between the demographic groups it presumes to straddle. In the present section, I argue that the portraiture of agricultural workers in Latin American countries performs a double duty for coffee companies. First, it allows maximum public relations benefits from minimal participation in fair trade programs in a process discussed here as "fair washing." Second, the imagery serves as a guarantee that the Global North's elite is performing their due diligence for the agricultural

Other in the South, suggesting a pathway toward redemption of colonial oppression through consumption of highly priced coffee.

What we now call fair trade emerged from the Alternative Trading Organizations (ATOs) of the 1960s and '70s that began as church-related networks to create markets for the products of impoverished or displaced peoples.[33] In Europe, this work was first known as "alternative trade." "Trade not aid" was a rallying cry raised by groups that opposed the paternalism and foreign aid by and to governments. According to Pauline Tiffen, an early trade network activist, the name of the conference Who Cares About Fair Trade? probably led to the widespread adoption of the term as it is used today.[34]

From its origins as a labeling system that began in churches and activist networks, a watershed year for the recognition and standardization of fair trade in the United States took place in 1993, when a coalition of bird-habitat activists concerned about the Amazonian rainforest and alternative trade workers advocating for better conditions among producers affiliated with a German-based trade umbrella called TransFair International. In 1998 TransFair USA gained momentum, with coffee always providing the cornerstone of its label's success. With its corporate-centered approach, TransFair balanced its commitment to Third World solidarity movements with the language of corporate profitability. Although alternative traders typically called for a 5 percent volume of purchases as a minimal threshold for fair trade certification, TransFair signed an agreement with Starbucks in 2000 that amounted to less than 1 percent of Starbucks' purchases, with no commitment to incremental increases of fair trade product stipulated in the negotiation. According to Rosenthal (2011), the TransFair approach to certifying tends to dominate U.S. models, many of which take even gentler reform approaches in order to win acceptance from corporate licensees, with slow growth resulting not only from low corporate participation but also low consumer awareness.[35]

Certain patterns emerge when it comes to large corporations gaining access to fair trade certifications and labels. Starbucks, along with Proctor and Gamble (makers of Folgers) and Nestlé, has been found to maximize all possible public relations benefits of fair trade certifications, while limiting actual participation in fair trade practices to a few token exchanges. "Fair washing," or using fair trade certification on certain products as a marketing strategy rather than an ethical commitment to build better lives for rural workers and more sustainable agricultural practices, typifies the corporate approach to fair trade, while at the same time undermining its prospects as a social movement.

While it is far from perfect, fair trade benefits workers on several levels when compared with conventional production models. Fair trade policies offer guaranteed minimum wages; participants and cooperatives engaged in the fair trade supply chain report less financial indebtedness than their counterparts. Lateral benefits include increased levels of formal educational attainment among the children of fair trade coffee producers. Shade-grown coffee supports the biodiversity and sustainability of traditional agricultural practices and heritage foodsheds and provides an alternative to emigration in the regions where coffee producers can rely on price guarantees that withstand the uncertainties of market fluctuations. The downsides of fair trade include the increased cost of labor for producers, who must pay significantly more wages for the labor-intensive crops to maintain organic and fair trade certifications, and the rigors of regulations, including bureaucracies and middlemen with unyielding timelines that compromise the ability of producers to address issues that arise around production and labor in real time.[36]

While the fair trade program is, by any and all measures, a very imperfect solution to oppressive economic, political, and environmental practices, the support of fair trade certifications on the part of much wealthier consumers is extremely easy, amounting to purchasing a product that they were going to buy anyway but ensuring that the Fair Trade Certified seal is located on the bag of beans (or clothing, home goods, or an array of agricultural products). However, the absolute ease with which a fair trade certification lands in a grocery store cart or a cup of house blend for prices comparable to conventional products becomes obstructed by visual and discursive practices that distort the reality behind corporate commitments to ethical sources.

As defined by Fair Trade International,

> Fair trade is a trading partnership, based on dialogue, transparency, and respect, that seeks greater equity in international trade. It contributes to sustainable development by offering better trading conditions to, and securing the rights of, marginalized producers and workers—

especially in the South. Fair Trade Organizations (backed by consumers) are actively engaged in supporting producers, in awareness raising and in campaigning for changes in the rules and practices of international trade.[37]

The "backed by consumers" phrase here is significant. In his study on the consumer and activist engagement with fair trade offerings, Brown (2013) draws on his own experiences with fellow travelers who participated in a homestay program with fair trade producers in Nicaragua to understand how face-to-face experience with artisans and coffee workers had fundamentally changed their understanding of fair trade programs. "Instead of reciting facts about the benefits of fair trade, most of them focused on a memorable experience meeting a fair-trade farmer or artisan. These encounters had convinced them that they had seen for themselves how their actions as shoppers can make a difference in the world."[38] Empathy sprang from their travels and firsthand exchanges with producer hosts, playing with their young children, undergoing exhaustion after a day of picking coffee berries alongside malnourished children, and being exposed to poor sanitation and mosquitoes carrying malaria and dengue fever. Once internalized via participatory observation, their travels led to increased advocacy for fair trade products and the urgency behind making consumer choices that benefited producers abroad.

The photography of rural producers displayed in coffeehouses in urban settings across the United States should, ostensibly, serve as a substitute for this firsthand experience of the extremely hard work that goes into the "perfect cup." While visitors to Nicaraguan coffee farms were convinced of the potential of fair trade to reshape the marketplace and thereby create a more socially just world order, the auxiliary "presence" of rural workers in elite spaces help to convince purchasers that they have, at the point of sale, done their part to achieve solidarity coffee. However, these portraits may actually be doing the opposite by lulling consumers into a false sense that fair trade commitments have been met, and lives have been improved, when this is not the case.

Third wave coffee representatives from companies such as Intelligentsia and Counter Culture tend to reject the fair trade certification system and opt, instead, for direct trade relationships. Intelligentsia, for example, takes pride in their direct trading relationships with farmers and pay prices that are even higher than what fair trade certification standards require. However, regulation of the quality of coffee, rather than growing conditions, is the priority of direct trade relationships, while fair trade protects farmers from price fluctuations, and emphasizes work with small farming cooperatives. Direct trade, unlike fair trade, is not a form of certification but a narrow focus on the values important to a given company. By subscribing to direct trade, large companies such as Starbucks, Intelligentsia, and Blue Apron end up competing with, rather than contributing to, the potential of the fair trade movement to create lasting change for producers.[39]

And even within fair trade organizations not all certifications share the same values. A lack of trust in Fair Trade USA, which ended its relationship with Fair Trade International in 2011, comes primarily from the low standards of its corporate participants. United Students for Fair Trade formally withdrew its support for Fair Trade USA in 2011, citing plantation sourcing, unacceptable "blends" of Fair Trade products with non–Fair Trade (as low as 11 percent Fair Trade content while still enjoying the marketing benefits of Fair Trade labeling), and conflicts of interests in funding of certifiers among many other issues with Transfair / Fair Trade USA's practices.[40] For multinational companies and their shareholders who try to skirt fair trade movement demands, the only force that can compel practices toward more just and equitable partnerships with growers inevitably comes from consumer pressure, but the problem is that consumers do not ask for what they believe they already have.

Portraiture in corporate coffeehouses provides a sense of false vicariousness for consumers. Rather than the intimacy experienced by "reality tour" travelers to Nicaraguan fair trade coffee producers, the photography really is a substitute for, rather than a representation of, a commitment to fair trade's values and goals. By fair washing through the symbolic presence of the gratified faces of coffee laborers, consumers are invited to imagine that the high premiums they are willing to pay for their perfect cup are benefiting the Mexicans, Ethiopians, Guatemalans, and Nicaraguans on display. In the staging of the sleek, corporate coffeehouse, displays stage the contiguity between consumer Northern publics and the agricultural Other. In Edenic configurations of human subjects set among verdant coffee plants, coffeehouse walls lined with portraits of producers suggest the accurate witnessing of a given establishment's participation in the improvement of the producers' life chances.

Along with fair washing, a simultaneous semiotic encounter takes place that helps to entrench the ideology of the noblesse oblige. As we have seen, the juxtaposition of coffee products and portraits of "remote" coffee workers provides symbolic assurances of social responsibility. This means that the indulgence in the high aesthetic (and high price) of third wave coffee is not only a sign of elite discernment but also an obligation of the wealthy patron class, who are expected to give back to their inferiors. The concept of the noble duty to the poor is described in Pierre Bourdieu's *Distinction* (1984).[41] Characterized by the requirement that the wealthy "live up" to their category, this generosity required by the noblesse oblige converts the relationship between Third World agricultural workers into proof of the benevolence of their patrons toward them (Mexicans, Guatemalans, Ethiopians, and so on). As in ancient Athens, as described below by Jennifer Tolbert Roberts, a steady patronage of various aspects of public life was the expectation of the dominant class:

> The wealthy were regularly assigned public burdens known as liturgies. The variety of possible liturgies reflects the vibrancy of cultural life at Athens; they included not only outfitting warships but also holding banquets and training choruses for dramatic performances. The rich were understandably ambivalent about exercising this sort of "privilege"; noblesse oblige could be very expensive.[42]

With high-end coffee, the obligation to help the poor has been fused to the elite mandate to consume with discernment the products of the highest quality. The art patrons of coffee, these curatorial stewards of the finest beans, are distinct from the unwashed imbibers: it is imperative not only to be an aesthete but also to ensure that this privilege performs double duty as a charitable act as well.

If Starbucks shops and latte consumption are widely held to be the territory of elite consumers, Blue Bottle Coffee is geared toward an even more exclusive clientele. I include a discussion of Blue Bottle here not because their ad campaigns are known to feature imagery of third world agricultural workers but because any interpretation of the relationship between third wave coffee consumption and coffee labor in Latin America and Africa is predicated on an understanding of gourmet coffee's political positionality as expressed by its architects and trendsetters. And by all measures, the decadence most uniformly associated with third wave coffee consumption is epitomized by Blue Bottle Coffee's owner and founder, James Freeman.

Journalists seem to delight in coming up with Blue Bottle descriptors that equate the enterprise and its rarified world with something akin to the decadent pleasures of ancien regime aristocracy. Freeman's own commitment to ethical sourcing and his application of meticulous craft behind Blue Bottle's offerings seem benign enough. Referring to the preparation at each stage of this chain as a "ritual," he emphasizes the connections across all stages of coffee provisioning in a way that is evocative of Alice Waters's commitment to farm-to-table dining: "I love the chain between the grower, and the roaster, and the barista, and the customer," says Freeman in his trailer for *The Blue Bottle Craft of Coffee: Growing, Roasting, and Drinking, with Recipes* (2012). Taken at face value, Freeman's approach seems progressive and inclusive, bringing the growers and farmworkers into the narrative of his success. But the tone of popular reactions, such as that of Joel Stein for *Bloomberg*, convey strong disgust with every minute aspect of Freeman's participation in the coffee industry, from his hip but professional haircut, to his Mr. Rogers cardigan sweater, to the "caring" his company strives to convey with surgically simple storefronts:

> You cannot order your espresso to go, choose a beverage size, or get your bag of coffee beans pre-ground. Oh no. This is not because Freeman wants to inform you of his superior ways but because he can't bear to be responsible for an imperfect experience. Because he so deeply cares.[43]

And from Josh Ozersky for *Time*:

> These guys see coffee not just as a hot beverage to drink in the morning, but as a way of life, an attitude toward the world, a spiritual direction and, most importantly,

Figure 6. Blue Bottle moments.

a passionate political statement about how to strive for
a better world. Which is why everybody wants to kill
them.[44]

Here is the propensity to see Freeman as the personification of the
cultural divide between the "Dunkin' Doughnuts" coffee drinker and
the "Starbucks liberals" against which not only members of the GOP,
but also anyone with an aversion to blatant status products, rails.

Figure 7. Starbucks donates a coffee tree to farmers for every brewed Mexico Chiapas on National Coffee Day.

Particularly significant in the above quotes is the equivalency be-tween high-end coffee products and the notion of "caring" and striv-ing for a "better world." The noble aesthete is prompted to confide in the ethical commitment of a given establishment by the discursive and photographic "evidence" of the contentment of mestizo and indige-nous agricultural workers.

In the above image from the Starbucks website, which is repre-sentative of much of the portraiture that hangs in their brick-and-mortar dining areas, the coffee plant in the foreground is sharp and clearly defined, occupying the visual place of privilege in the frame. In blurred lines, but clearly discernable, the face of the worker corrob-orates with the photographer's focal point. With a rapt and admiring gaze, the worker holds up the infant plant in a gesture of wonderment that borders on spiritual devotion. The close-up on the plant places the two subjects in perfect alignment with the tenets of moderniza-tion theory: we see the entire agricultural subject, with the blurred human subject in service to agricultural subject, holding it above eye-level in clear reverence.

In all accounts describing the importance and impact of fair trade, the pressure exerted by consumers—not governments, corporations, or nonprofit organizations—is what drives corporations to make changes in their business practices that help producers in the South move out of the devastation of poverty to which cash crop economies in forcibly underdeveloped countries are subject. But, owing to the rampant practice of fair washing, consumers are made to believe that they are taking part in a movement by buying in at the high price points associated with second and third wave coffee's marketing systems, thereby limiting the political awareness that shapes consumer advocacy for fair trade programs. These rarified corridors of caffeinated refinement convince consumers they have satisfied the directive of their status by providing the agricultural Other with a route to economic security by allowing them to do what is framed as traditional, spiritual, ancestral, and natural: serving the elites of the North.

Good Morning, Latinidad!

So far I've detailed the performative context of Juan Valdez, whose enduring legacy as a beloved Colombian icon crosses ideological borders when he takes root in the U.S. popular imagination as the colonial fantasy of the agricultural Other, and demonstrated how marketing systems incorporate portraiture and discursive practices to lull the consumer into imagining that they have fulfilled their elite obligation to both consume the finest product and expiate class privilege at the point of sale by purchasing their cup. I turn now to the impact of the visual campaign featuring mestizo agricultural workers and its impact on the construction of public identities of Latino customers at the receiving end of the marketing machinery that locates Latin Americans as remote, indigent, and subservient.

Marketing communications pioneer Tom Burrell has long combated stereotypes and racism in advertising by countering Black inferiority with positive and realistic images of African Americans in television advertising. Referring to the pervasive marketing of Black inferiority as "the greatest propaganda campaign of all time," the generational legacy of slavery and the logic that permitted its foundational institutionalization in this country remains rampant.

"So this whole idea that we're talking about ancient history, we're talking about a few generations ago. And these traditions, this inferiority that was drummed into us through the media, through propaganda, has passed down from generation to generation just like a favorite family recipe."[45] As remarked above, Black potential has been obstructed by food industry propaganda that naturalizes racial inferiority through the omnipresence of caricatures such as Uncle Ben, Rastus, and Aunt Jemima that, as Kern-Foxworth points out, were made to seem docile, ignorant, and ugly. While portraiture of indigeneity and mestizaje in the coffee shops may not be on the same level as the overtly racist eyesores such as Frito Bandito, Chiquita Banana, and the Taco Bell Chihuahua, they must be flagged for being dangerous in their own way. Along with that morning coffee, dichotomous promotional materials hail Northern elite consumers in one way, while saying something entirely different to people of Latin American origin. The permanent staging of coffee-producing mestizo bodies as both remote and racially subservient, this visual strategy is designed appeal to Whites, while reminding Latinos of their "place."

First, let's look at the evidence that lets us know that mestizos are not the target audience for the images such as the photograph above. Fixed in frames as either gleeful or solemn harvesters, the only images of mestizo subjects I could find in the coffee house dining areas at Starbucks across the country are performing agricultural labor, but never shown as consumers. While recent Starbucks video advertisements tend to feature young, trendy consumers and baristas, none of the markers of advertising for Latino publics are present. As Dávila has pointed out, the major tropes in Hispanic marketing include cultural comparisons that either depict Latino achievement, urge Latinos to enjoy the conveniences of modernity, showcase "Latin looks," and/or frame the traditional family as the definitive source of meaning in Latino lives. However, in-store visual references and the live action commercials I was able to access do not draw on any of these conventions and only reference mestizo and indigenous peoples as inseparable from the activities of harvest. The spate of racist incidents at Starbucks stores nationwide further attests to the brand's propensity to exclusively hail White consumers.

The second wave explosion of coffee culture, along with its attending exclusion of U.S. Latinidad, has not been subtle, and it has not gone unremarked. Lalo Alcaraz's "Café Attitudo" provides a Chicano-facing insider awareness of the class- and race-based exclusivity associated with coffeehouses. The cartoon's "You're NEVER welcome" loudly declares what perceptive Latinos already hear. I first encountered the comic strip hanging in a frame on the wall of Chicago's Jumping Bean Café, a stalwart of the Mexican American neighborhood of Pilsen where I lived for eight years. Not only the Alcaraz strip but also the irony of the coffee shop's name (historically, "jumping bean" has been used as a racial slur, which is reclaimed by the Mexican American dining establishment), both swipe at the usual coffeehouse ethos that seems to always be sneering and looking down on its clientele.

Although the comic strip could not be called an "ad," it yet serves to communicate the public identity that Jumping Bean wishes to share with its customers: self-ironic, anti-elitist, and pro-Chicano. The circulation of inside jokes about Mexican national rejection strikes a chord with community members who experience the consequences of racism, while also employing humor as a strategy of empowerment and neighborhood camaraderie. Spatial exclusion is made clear by the cartoon's weekly calendar posted behind the irascible barista: Monday's "Restricted Mike Night," Thursday's "Folk Off," Friday's "Melrose Place Night," Saturday's "UCLA Frat Nite," and Sunday's "Indignant

Figure 8. Café Attitudo. Cartoon by Lalo Alcaraz.

White Poetry Nite" articulate the insider cognizance of who third wave coffee houses are intended to appeal to. This "private joke" moment is, according to advertising executive Christopher Davis, the distinguishing characteristic of marketing endeavors that appeal to people of color.

> Good minority ads, on the other hand, are the opposite of blatant. . . . Rather than using cultural cues that are obvious to outsiders, they show subtle understanding and an insider's affinity with the audience's background. "Minority insights are based on a lifetime of cultural absorption and several years of craft," says True executive creative director Christopher Davis. . . . "They are like a private joke that takes a lifetime to tell."[46]

At Café Jumping Bean, Alcaraz's artwork represents a tacit understanding shared by Latinos: in second and third wave coffee houses, servers want brown customers to have their coffee TO GO!

The spatial messages about where Latinos "belong" is both hidden in plain sight and heavily coded, and recent occurrences at Starbucks stores in which White employees call police to remove Black customers while portraits of Ethiopian harvesters decorate the walls and coffee bags attest to the coffeehouse state of affairs. The geographies filling the frames of agricultural portraiture are consistently associated with the national origin of a given bean. Single origin beans from Colombia, Nicaragua, or Mexico follow in the Juan Valdez model of joining pride of place to satisfaction with servitude and the knowledge that the best product is for export to the North. The physical remoteness of the worker is emphasized by the natural surroundings, sending a message about the relationship between mestizo bodies and their proximity to the natural world. Given that youthful urbanites are the strategic target of Starbucks' marketing energies, the contrast is striking. The agricultural and racial Other is always grateful to his or her hemispheric overlords for the opportunity to continue in their ancestral vocation of plucking coffee berries for Whites.

Following Burrell and Berg, massified forms of media hold powerful sway in the manufacture of public identities, naturalizing their participation in work that is dirty, dangerous, and difficult:

> If members of a group are consistently portrayed in low
> status occupations, this may lead society at large to a be-
> lief that members of the group are not intelligent enough,
> or not diligent enough, to hold higher status jobs.[47]

The romantic and pastoral images that solidify a mythical connection between mestizo and indigenous workers and agricultural activity not only seem inoffensive but appear to be progressive and innovative in their promise of raising coffee producers out of poverty. However, these portraits participate in the same racial scripts that propel the Chiquita Banana and Cream of Wheat Rastus onto the breakfast table, albeit with an aesthetic update to suit the interior design scheme of the local Starbucks.

CONCLUSION

Big Vehicle Food Fight

In the chapters of *Food Fight! Millennial Mestizaje Meets the Culinary Marketplace*, I have endeavored to look closely at some of the practices, discourses, and image systems that characterize the national culinary marketplace. In "Farmworker-to-Table Mexican: Decolonizing Haute Cuisine," I call for greater accountability to the rights of farmworkers in the farm-to-table movement, while challenging cultural biases that obstruct the dignified integration of mestizo and indigenous peoples into the world of fine dining. "On Cinco de Drinko and Jimmiechangas: Culinary Brownface in the Rust Belt Midwest" interprets the presence of Mexican-styled restaurants that continue to draw on colonial stereotypes, while heritage cooks, servers, and patrons employ strategies of adaptive authenticity to maintain heritage foods alongside a nonheritage customer base. Next, my chapters "Homegirl Café: La Conciencia Mestiza as Culinary Counterstory" and "From Juan Valdez to Third Wave Cafés: Lattes and Latinidad in the Marketplace" investigate the travels of mestizaje and Latinidad in commercial media representations, with the "Homegirl" chapter emphasizing the Chicana feminist embrace of the chola signifier, and the latter interrogating coffee image systems featuring Latin American, indigenous, and mestizo bodies that are used by corporate campaigns to reinforce economic models of dependency.

But more than the sum of the specific arguments I make in each of the chapters, *Food Fight!* represents just a small fractal in the ongoing struggle to resist the logics and behaviors by which our planet and its most vulnerable peoples are the victims of unsustainable and inequitable standards in our food-provisioning systems. Unfortunately for everyone, there is no shortage of places to take a stand, and these frontlines in the fight against poverty, discrimination, and irresponsible development range well beyond what there is room to discuss within the front and back covers of this book. My intention has been to offer a Chicana mestiza perspective on some of the areas of our foodways that are plainly pathological, when not unmistakably apocalyptic. A recent estimate calculates that a reeling 8 million metric tons of plastic pollution enter the oceans each year,[1] largely composed of the abandoned fishing gear, plastic bags from grocery stores, soda can rings, plastic bottles, food wrappers, and single-use straws that represent how we catch, package, and consume food. These plastics have devastating effects on fish, seabirds, turtles, and other marine creatures, which become the victims of plastic ingestion. To narrow the focus to just one item stocked and distributed throughout the dining industry, a recent estimate tells us that the United States goes through about 175 million single-use straws every single day,[2] while beef, soy, and palm oil are among the top products driving tropical deforestation. On the national level, the Western pattern diet or Standard American Diet (SAD), characterized by preferences for red and processed meat, fried foods, and high-sugar drinks, is associated with the increased risk of chronic diseases along with inadequate intakes of essential nutrients. In other words, the SAD diet's victims are both overfed and undernourished—both starving and obese. It's also sobering to learn that, according to the United Nations Environment Programme, one third of all food produced in the world (about 1.3 billion tons) is lost or wasted every year, and food waste is responsible for more than 7 percent of the world's greenhouse gas emissions, constituting the largest volume of materials in U.S. landfills.[3] At the same time, widespread food insecurity, or the phenomenon of households uncertain or unable to acquire enough food to meet the needs of all their family members, affected 815 million people (about 11 percent of the global population) in 2016, according United Nations reports.[4] In the United States, one of the richest countries in the world based on average household income, the percentage is even higher: about 12.3 percent (15.6 million) of U.S. households were food insecure at some point in 2016.[5] And this stark list of realities encompassing domestic and international tragedies related to food security and environmental destruction could go on and on. And on.

Given these troubling realities that define our moment as social and civic actors at the planetary level, what can mestizaje hope to provide? What claims can—*must*—this corner of the ring contribute to the fight? In this book's pages, the goal has been to apply the optics of cultural analysis to help us discern the specific ways in which people of indigenous and Latin American extraction are the targets, and survivors, of oppressive colonial food chains, as iterated in today's marketplace through the logic of neoliberal policies and colonial and patriarchal fantasies.

My experience at the Wendy's 2018 Annual Meeting of Stockholders that took place in Dublin, Ohio, provides a telling example. I had been asked by the Coalition of Immokalee Workers (CIW) to provide remarks about working conditions in the agricultural industry in Mexico to address Wendy's preferential purchasing of tomatoes south of the border. Earlier that morning we had gathered at Panera Bread to coordinate our entry into the stockholder's meeting and establish an order of speakers to raise questions in front of the gathered officers and shareholders. At Panera I sat at a small table with CIW members Lusvi, Nely, and don Andrés, as well as Marco, a first-year student attending the University of North Carolina at Chapel Hill. We talked about the need not only to tell the stories of farmworkers but to raise the social intelligence and compassion among consumers who have no contact with the labor that goes into the harvest of tomato, squash, peppers, and other produce that appear, as though by magic, on their family's dining table. I brought up how, at the grocery store, people are anxious to find the deepest discount available, but they are willing to spend more on status symbols when, for example, it's a clothing logo or a new pair of sneakers that says something about their identity. In other words, consumers in the West are enthusiastic to pay more if a product is viewed as a status purchase. How can we convince consumers to attach this kind of symbolic value to the dignity and life chances of their food's producers? A university education, noted Lusvi, tells people about the idea of how food reaches consumers, but not the reality. The CIW members I spoke with believed that if young people spent just one day in the fields picking crops, they would have an entirely different understanding of the food supply chain and the significance of consumer responsibility in creating a different world.

The conversation ended when it was time to head to Wendy's headquarters a short drive away. Following recommendations of CIW organizers, I wore "business formal" attire: a navy skirt suit, heels, and a shoulder bag, rather than the gym shoes and backpack more characteristic of my summer wardrobe. The idea was to trickle in, rather than arrive as a group, so that board members and shareholders would not prevent us from entering and having a voice during the final question and answer portion of the meeting. The members of the CIW, it was decided in advance, would enter together, as the group of Spanish-dominant agricultural workers with dark complexions represented a clearly delineated and unified block in the rarified space of Anglo-dominant corporate privilege.

Long-time organizer Gerardo Reyes Chávez, a farmworker since the age of eleven, joined the CIW shortly after his arrival to the United States in 2000. Reyes has helped investigate several human trafficking operations, including performing undercover work on tomato farms and interviewing workers to expose brutal modern-day slavery operations.[6] Reyes was the first CIW member to speak, and he addressed board members and shareholders about the Fair Food Program's value as the widely recognized gold standard of social responsibility. As we learned in that day's presentation by Wendy's chief communications officer, they plan to repatriate 90 percent of their tomato purchases to the United States in contracts with greenhouse growers. However, as CIW members pointed out, greenhouse workers face the same abuses, harassment, violence, and forced labor as their counterparts working outside.

After hearing from Reyes, Wendy's chairman of the board Nelson Peltz refused to call on any other members of the CIW. It was evident that there were many other representatives with their hands up, but they were excluded from the conversation. It appeared that my dark suit had been the right choice, as Peltz called on me to ask the last question of the day. I used the opportunity to explain that, as a professor at the Ohio State University, I was joined by colleagues and students to oppose the university's contract with Wendy's while they remain connected to the abuse of worker's rights. But I felt shame in having been granted the opportunity to speak while important Fair Food Program organizers had not, owing to the color and class lines drawn throughout the room, and across our faces, bodies, and life chances. The CIW's Lupe Gonzalo and Nely Rodriguez were two female leaders whose hands had been raised in the meeting and ignored. Later in the day, they had the chance to share their thoughts about Wendy's new decision to move tomato harvests to greenhouse operations at a gathering of organizers and allies at the Methodist Theological School in Ohio (MTSO), following the shareholder's meeting. There, Gonzalo clarified her position on the repatriation of the tomato harvest:

> The reality is that workers in greenhouses face the very same situations of abuse, and sometimes it's even worse than in an open field. Sometimes, people think of greenhouses in the way they think about organic food—the tomato sounds like it will be of a higher quality, and so the working conditions must also be better. But it's not just about having organic food on the table, or even just about saying that workers have shade and therefore all of their problems are solve—it's about ensuring actual human rights. But Wendy's isn't going to see or understand that, because they once again are sitting inside in their offices, dreaming up the quality of life that farmworkers supposedly have.[7]

The CIW members and representatives were all acutely aware of the politics of visibility, representation, and exclusion at the shareholders' meeting, and the difference between the people making decisions about working conditions and the people actually performing the work. Over and over again, the White members of the audience with their hands up were selected by Peltz to approach the mic, while Gonzalo, Rodriguez, and other CIW workers were silenced. Considering the fact that, in 2010 the United States Department of Labor reported that 77 percent of the nation's crop workers were of Mexican and Central American origin, the decision to permit only one crop worker's voice in the room was telling. As the agricultural and dining industries depend on this predominantly mestizo labor force, accountable advocacy for food justice must take into account the majoritarian stories that oppress and dehumanize workers of Latin American and indigenous cultures in historically and culturally specific patterns that I have examined here.

Even so, mestizaje as a political and theoretical vehicle for transformation of our foodways has some significant limitations. CIW organizers were surprised to discover that Reverend Jesse Jackson was also in attendance at the Wendy's shareholder's meeting, and he was the next to speak after Reyes. He addressed the board as a customer, opening his remarks with praise for the "homestyle chicken sand-wich," before raising the problem of the wealth gap in the United States, explaining that more than half of all Americans earn less than fifteen dollars an hour, while the costs of education and transportation have far outpaced wage growth. Although Reyes and Jackson had shared a microphone on the floor of the shareholder's meeting, their context for worker advocacy was formed by colonial trajectories that manufacture racial hostility in different ways for different subjects. As president and CEO at Wendy's, Todd A. Penegor made $5,117,784 in the 2016 fiscal year. At the meeting seated at the dais, he and Nelson Peltz were both complicit in ignoring the raised hands of the many CIW members present, but Peltz also followed Jackson's remarks with something along the lines of a guttural, "Gotta have that chicken" comment that elicited a round of laughs from his target audience. My thought at the time was, *No, you do not get to do an "Mmm, chicken" voice with Jesse Jackson.* Following Jackson's address with jocular familiarity and racially coded "humor," the Wendy's CEO provided a reminder that African American communities deal with food insecurity, wage stagnation, nutrition-related disease loads, and dehumanizing colonial fantasies throughout the food provisioning system in unique ways that mestizaje does not begin to address. Big vehicle transformation of our foodways—meaning everyone can get in—must take place through dialogue and strategies that acknowledge shared humanity across color lines, while taking stock of the varying strategies corporate food chains deploy to quarantine the agency—and maximize the exploitation—of people of color.

A heartening moment took place after the meeting outside of the corporate headquarters, as Reverend Jackson and his retinue joined hands with Immokalee workers and Fair Food Program advocates in a prayer. Jackson's devotional words resonate strongly with the impetus and energies that brought me to write this book, so I include them here: "Give us the strength to fight the fight. It's the right fight. Touch our hearts to make us better, never bitter. And we will not give up, we will not surrender."

Jackson's Rainbow Coalition cohort and members of the CIW parted affectionately after the prayer, and CIW organizers continued on to the lunch being held at the MTSO seminary, where the Immokalee group was being hosted. There, Reyes proudly reported about the surprise encounter with Reverend Jackson, "Me dio el secret hand-shake!" But his tone became serious again when he confirmed to the assembled visitors that there were no small actions in the movement for farmworkers' rights, and its success does not depend on the decisions made by Wendy's executives, but on us. Describing the individual and collective efforts to advance protections through the auspices of the Fair Food Program, "Every action is a drop of water," Reyes said. "The rock thinks that it's unbreakable, but that drop of water is going to keep striking until it breaks through to the core." At the shareholder's meeting, it was never more apparent to me that workers and consumers have the power to reshape our foodways when knowledge and compassion are joined to persistent action. Graced to be in the presence of so many courageous fighters on the front line of the fight for food justice, Reyes's words reinvigorated my conviction that, while we can't do all things right each and every day, no day goes by that we can't do *one* thing. Knuckles up.

NOTES

Introduction

1. "Mestizaje," *Oxford Dictionaries*, accessed December 3, 2017, https://en .oxforddictionaries.com/definition/mestizaje.

2. Sheila Contreras, *Blood Lines: Myth, Indigenism, and Chicana/o Literature* (Austin: University of Texas Press, 2008); Deborah Pacini Hernandez, *Oye Como Va! Hybridity and Identity in Latin American Popular Music* (Philadelphia: Temple University Press, 2010), 8.

3. Josefina Saldaña-Portillo, "Who's the Indian in Aztlán: Re-writing Mestizaje, Indianism, and Chicanismo from the Lacandón," in *The Latin American Subaltern Studies Reader*, ed. Ileana Rodríguez (Durham: Duke University Press, 2001).

4. Rafael Pérez-Torres, *Mestizaje: Critical Uses of Race in Chicano Culture* (Minneapolis: University of Minnesota Press, 2006), 13.

5. Peter Wade et al., "Genomics, Race Mixture, and Nation," in *Mestizo Genomics: Race Mixture, Nation, and Science in Latin America* (Durham: Duke University Press, 2014), 1–30.

6. Contreras, *Blood Lines*, 9–37.

7. Pérez-Torres, *Mestizaje*, 24.

8. Gloria Anzaldúa, *Borderlands / La Frontera: The New Mestiza*, 3rd ed. (San Francisco: Aunt Lute Books, 2007), 73.

9. Edwina Barvosa, *Wealth of Selves: Multiple Identities, Mestiza Consciousness, and the Subject of Politics* (Austin: University of Texas Press, 2008), 55.

10. Denise A. Segura and Beatriz M. Pesquera, "Beyond Indifference and Antipathy: The Chicana Movement and Chicana Feminist Discourse," *Aztlán Journal* 19, no. 2 (1992): 69–93.

11. Sonia Saldivar-Hull, "Feminism on the Border: From Gender Politics to Geopolitics," in *Criticism in the Borderlands: Studies in Chicano Literature, Culture and Ideology*, eds. Hector Calderon and Jose David Saldivar (Durham: Duke University Press, 1991).

12. Chela Sandoval, "Mestizaje as Method: Feminists-of-Color Challenge the Canon," in *Living Chicana Theory*, ed. Carla Trujillo (Berkeley: Third Woman Press, 1998), 355.

13. Cristina Beltrán, *The Trouble with Unity: Latino Politics and the Creation of Identity* (Oxford: Oxford University Press, 2010).

14. Aníbal Quijano, "Coloniality of Power, Eurocentrism, and Latin America," *Nepantla: Views from South* 1, no. 3 (2000): 535.

15. Louis McFarland, *The Chican@ Hip Hop Nation* (East Lansing: Michigan State University Press, 2013), 9.

16. Laura Pulido, *Environmentalism and Economic Justice: Two Chicano Struggles in the Southwest* (Tucson, University of Arizona Press, 1996); Julie Guthman. *The Paradox of Organic Farming in California*, 2nd ed. (Oakland: University of California Press, 2014).

17. Jennifer Smith Richards, "Hispanics Lead Population Growth in Ohio," *Columbus Dispatch*, June 26, 2014, http://www.dispatch.com/content/stories/local/2014/06/26/hispanics-lead-state-population-increases.html.

Chapter 1

1. Sam Oches, "Special Report," *QSR Magazine*, August 8, 2013.

2. Juan Gonzalez, *Harvest of Empire: A History of Latinos in America* (New York: Penguin Books, 2011), 216.

3. United States Department of Agriculture Economic Research Service, last modified May 2, 2018, https://www.ers.usda.gov/topics/farm-economy/farm-labor/#legalstatus.

4. Jeffrey Pilcher, *Que vivan los tamales!* (Albuquerque: University of New Mexico Press, 1998), 4.

5. Amelia Lester, "Cosme," *New Yorker*, February 9, 2015, https://www.newyorker.com/magazine/2015/02/09/tables-two-19.

6. Quijano, "Coloniality of Power," 535.

7. "Chefs and Head Cooks," Data USA, https://datausa.io/profile/soc/351011/.

8. Zlati Meyer, "5 Reasons Why Restaurants Can Be Hotbeds of Sexual Harassment," *USA Today*, December 18, 2017, https://www.usatoday.com/story/money/2017/12/18/5-reasons-why-restaurants-can-hotbeds-sexual-harassment/950137001/.

9. Gustavo Arellano, *Taco USA: How Mexican Food Conquered America* (New York: Scribner, 2012); Michael Soldatenko, "Tacos and Coloniality: A Review Essay," *Diálogo: An Interdisciplinary Studies Journal* 18, no. 1 (2015): 136.

10. Meredith E. Abarca and Nieves Pascual Soler, *Rethinking Chicana/o Literature Through Food: Postnational Appetites* (New York: Palgrave Macmillan, 2013).

11. Jeffrey Pilcher, *Planet Taco: A Global History of Mexican Food* (Oxford: Oxford University Press, 2012).

12. José Antonio Burciaga, "After Aztlán," in *Undocumented Love / Amor Indocumentado* (San Jose, Calif.: Chusma House, 1992), 16.

13. Paul Martinez Pompa, "The Abuelita Poem," in *My Kill Adore Him* (Notre Dame: University of Notre Dame Press, 2009), 40–41.

14. Paloma Martinez-Cruz, *Women and Knowledge in Mesoamerica: From East L.A. to Anahuac* (Tucson: University of Arizona Press, 2011), 18–19.

15. Ilan Stavans, *Mexican-American Cuisine* (Santa Barbara, Calif.: Greenwood, 2011), 4.

16. Elizabeth Fitting, "Cultures of Corn and Anti-GMO Activism in Mexico and Columbia," *Food Activism: Agency, Democracy and Economy*, eds. Carole Counihan and Valeria Siniscalchi (New York: Bloomsbury, 2014).

17. Zilkia Janer, *Latino Food Culture* (Westport, Conn.: Greenwood Press, 2008), 25.

18. Janer, *Latino Food Culture*, 73.

19 Janer, *Latino Food Culture*, 55.

20. Stavans, *Mexican-American Cuisine*, ix.

21. "National Restaurant Association Reports Top Restaurant Menu Trends," *Food & Beverage Close-Up*, December 6, 2013.

22. Dan Barber, "What Farm-to-Table Got Wrong," *New York Times*, May 17, 2014.

23. Hannah Palmer Egan, "The 10 Best (Real) Farm-to-Table Restaurants in NYC," *Village Voice*, August 5, 2013.

24. Fair Food Standards Council, *Fair Food Program 2014 Annual Report*, January 27, 2016, http://www.fairfoodstandards.org.

25. Kevin Morgan, Terry Marsden, and Jonathan Murdoch, *Worlds of Food: Place, Power, and Provenance in the Food Chain* (New York: Oxford University Press, 2006), 2.

26. *The New Green Giants: Is Organic Better?* Dir. Ted Remerowski, October 3, 2015, http://www.cbc.ca/doczone/features/is-organic-better.

27. Daniel Faber, *The Struggle for Ecological Democracy: Environmental Justice Movements in the United States* (London: Guilford Press, 1998), 5–6.

28. "Pesticide Safety," Farmworker Justice, accessed December 18, 2017, https://www.farmworkerjustice.org/content/pesticide-safety.

29. Devon G. Peña, *Mexican Americans and the Environment: Tierra y Vida* (Tucson: University of Arizona Press, 2005), 121–22.

30. Zachiah Murray, *Mindfulness in the Garden: Zen Tools for Digging in the Dirt* (Berkeley: Parallax Press, 2012).

31. Seth Holmes, *Fresh Fruit, Broken Bodies: Migrant Farmworkers in the United States* (Berkeley: University of California Press, 2013), 89.

32. Silvia Giagnoni, *Fields of Resistance* (Chicago: Haymarket Books, 2011), 34.

33. Rosaura Sánchez, *Chicano Discourse: Socio-Historic Perspectives* (Houston: Arte Público Press, 1983), 9.

34. Rodolfo Acuña, *Occupied America: A History of Chicanos* (Uppersaddle River, N.J.: Pearson, 2015), 262.

35. Kelly Lytle Hernández, "The Crimes and Consequences of Illegal Immigration: A Cross-Border Examination of Operation Wetback, 1943 to 1954," *Western Historical Quarterly* 37 (Winter 2006): 421–44.

36. Luz Calvo, *Decolonize Your Diet*, accessed December 18, 2017, http://decolonizeyourdiet.org/.

37. Enrique C. Ochoa, "From Tortillas to Low-Carb Capitalism and Mexican Food in Los Angeles Since the 1920s," *Diálogo: An Interdisciplinary Studies Journal* 18, no. 1 (2015): 33–46.

38. Peña, *Mexican Americans*, 139–46.

39. Beltrán, *The Trouble with Unity*, 43.

40. Alan Warde, *Consumption, Food, and Taste* (London: Sage, 1997), 22.

41. Arellano, *Taco USA*, 90.

42. Farm to Table New Mexico, accessed January 24, 2015, https://www.farmtotablenm.org/?gclid=CjwKCAiAjuPRBRBxEiwAeQ2QPgnoCyROHedGg_ssrKnmuJ3XQPRxH6qo-qnj6gvnOiFSOIv2nDfcAhoClvgQAvD_BwE.

43. Rick Bayless, accessed January 15, 2015, http://www.rickbayless.com/.

44. Bayless.

45. Bayless.

46. Maria Elena Cepeda, "'Columbus Effect(s)': Chronology and Crossover in the Latin(o) Music 'Boom,'" *Discourse* 23, no. 1 (2001): 62–81.

47. Michel-Rolph Trouillot, *Silencing the Past: Power and the Production of History* (Boston: Beacon Press, 2015), 114.

48. Linda Tuhiwai Smith, *Decolonizing Methodologies: Research and Indigenous Peoples* (London: Zed Books, 2002).

49. Smith, *Decolonizing Methodologies*, 1.

50. Border Grill Modern Mexican, accessed April 13, 2016, http://www.bordergrill.com/.

51. Border Grill.

52. Jennifer Graue, "San Jose's Zona Rosa Serves Upscale, Farm-to-Table Mexican Cuisine," *San José Mercury News*, March 19, 2013.

53. Ryan Sutton, "Six Reasons Why Cosme Is One of NYC's Most Relevant New Restaurants," *New York Eater*, December 16, 2014.

54. Amelia Lester, "Cosme," *New Yorker*, February 9, 2015.

55. Edible School Yard Project, accessed April 15, 2015, https://edibleschool
yard.org/.

56. Thomas McNamee, Alice Waters, and Chez Panisse, *The Romantic, Impractical, Often Eccentric, Ultimately Brilliant Making of a Food Revolution* (New
York: Penguin Press, 2007), 347.

57. Rice-Cisneros, personal interview, July 28, 2014.

58. Abarca, Meredith E. and Nieves Pascual Soler. *Rethinking Chicana/o Literature through Food: Postnational Appetites.* New York: Palgrave Macmillan,
2013.

59. Abarca and Soler, *Rethinking Chicana/o Literature Through Food*, 1.

Chapter 2

1. "Chi-Chi's Inc. History," Funding Universe, accessed November 29, 2017,
http://www.fundinguniverse.com/company-histories/chi-chi-s-inc-history/.

2. "Chi Chi's: A Story of Salsa and Food Poisoning," *Surfing Pizza*, posted May 8,
2009, https://thesurfingpizza.com/2009/05/08/chi-chis/.

3. Vicki Passmore, "10 Retailers and Restaurants We Really Miss," *Daily Fi-
nance*, November 2, 2010, https://www.aol.com/2010/11/02/10-retailers-and
-restaurants-we-really-miss/.

4. Rachel Sussman, "The Carnavalizing of Race," *Etnofoor* 14, no. 2 (2001).

5. "Lima, Ohio," City-Data.com, accessed November 29, 2017, http://www.city
-data.com/city/Lima-Ohio.html.

6. Janet Reitman, "Where the Tea Party Rules," *Rolling Stone*, http://www
.rollingstone.com/politics/news/where-the-tea-party-rules-20141014.

7. "Current Lima, Ohio Population, Demographics and Stats in 2016, 2017,"
Suburban Stats, accessed November 29, 2017, https://suburbanstats.org
/population/ohio/how-many-people-live-in-lima.

8. Douglas Walker, "Indiana Meth Lab Capital Has No Challengers," *Muncie
Star Press*, July 28, 2015, http://www.indystar.com/story/news/crime/2015
/07/28/indiana-meth-lab-capital-has-no-challengers/30771469/.

9. "Indiana Crowned Meth Capital of United States," Tristate Homepage, April 1,
2014, http://www.tristatehomepage.com/news/indiana-crowned-meth-capital
-of-united-states.

10. John Stehr, "Indiana's War on Meth—Part 2," 13 Eyewitness News, https://
www.wthr.com/article/indianas-war-on-meth-part-2.

11. "Terre Haute Population and Demographics," AreaConnect, accessed November 29, 2017, http://terrehaute.areaconnect.com/statistics.htm.

12. Joseph J. Varga, "Breaking the Heartland: Creating the Precariat in the US Lower Rust Belt," *Global Discourse: An Interdisciplinary Journal of Current Affairs and Applied Contemporary Thought* 3, nos. 3–4 (2013).

13. Robert Guell and Kevin Christ, "Terre Haute Forecast 2015," *Indiana Business Review* 89, no. 4 (Winter 2014), http://www.ibrc.indiana.edu/ibr/2014/outlook/terrehaute.html.

14. Mary Louise Pratt, *Imperial Eyes: Travel Writing and Transculturation* (New York: Taylor and Francis, 1992), 6–7.

15. Janer, Zilkia. *Latino Food Culture*. Westport, CT: Greenwood Press, 2008, 73.

16. Arellano, *Taco USA*.

17. Sussman, "The Carnavalizing of Race," 81.

18. Maria Godoy, "Why Hunting Down 'Authentic Ethnic Food' Is a Loaded Proposition," NPR, April 9, 2016, http://www.npr.org/sections/thesalt/2016/04/09/472568085/why-hunting-down-authentic-ethnic-food-is-a-loaded-proposition.

19. Arellano, *Taco USA*.

20. Carolina Miranda, "The California Taco Trail: 'How Mexican Food Conquered America,'" NPR, April 23, 2012, http://www.npr.org/sections/thesalt/2012/04/23/150886690/the-california-taco-trail-how-mexican-food-conquered-america.

21. Marc Lacey, "Arizonans Vie to Claim Cross-Cultural Fried Food," *New York Times*, November 15, 2011, http://www.nytimes.com/2011/11/16/us/arizonans-vie-to-claim-cross-cultural-fried-food.html?_r=0.

22. Arellano, *Taco USA*, 72.

23. Arellano, *Taco USA*, 139–49.

24. Virginia B. Wood, "Fajita History," *Austin Chronicle*, March 4, 2005, https://www.austinchronicle.com/food/2005-03-04/261130/.

25. "The Best 10 Mexican Restaurants in Lima, OH," Yelp, accessed June 10, 2016, https://www.yelp.com/search?cflt=mexican&find_loc=Lima%2C+OH.

26. Russell Cobb, ed. *The Paradox of Authenticity in a Globalized World* (New York: Palgrave Macmillan), xiii.

27. Josée Johnston and Shyon Baumann, *Foodies: Democracy and Distinction in the Gourmet Foodscape* (New York: Routledge, 2010), 100.

28. Charles Ramirez Berg, *Latino Images in Film: Stereotypes, Subversion, and Resistance* (Austin: University of Texas Press, 2002), 4.

29. Cepeda, "Columbus Effect(s)."

30. Beth Stallings, "The 12 Hottest New Restaurants in Columbus, Ohio," Eater, June 20, 2017, https://www.eater.com/maps/best-new-columbus-restaurants-heatmap.

31. G. A. Benton, "Cosecha Cocina: Mexican Meets Modern with Fresh, Delicious Results," *Columbus Alive*, May 18, 2017, http://www.columbusalive.com /entertainmentlife/20170518/restaurant-review-cosecha-cocina-mexican -meets-modern-with-fresh-delicious-results.

32. "Harvest a la Mexicana," (614) The Users Guide to Columbus, http://614 columbus.com/2016/12/harvest-a-la-mexicana/.

33. Sonya Fix, Facebook post, April 2, 2017.

34. Rice-Cisneros, personal interview, November 24, 2017.

Chapter 3

1. The Sentencing Project, accessed February 17, 2017, http://www.sentencing project.org/.

2. Angela Davis, "The Prison Industrial Complex," in *Civil Rights Since 1787: A Reader on the Black Struggle*, eds. Jonathan Birnbaum and Clarence Taylor (New York: New York University Press, 2000).

3. Akhila L. Ananth and Carly B. Dierkhising, *CURE Diversion Program: Process Evaluation Report* (Coalition for Responsible Community Development, 2015), 7.

4. Segura and Pesquera, "Beyond Indifference and Antipathy."

5. Saldivar-Hull, "Feminism on the Border."

6. Sandoval, "Mestizaje as Method," 355.

7. Sandoval, "Mestizaje as Method," 362.

8. James Lockhart, *Nahuatl as Written: Lessons in Older Written Nahuatl, with Copious Examples and Texts* (Stanford: Stanford University Press and UCLA Latin American Studies, 2001), 225.

9. Pati Zarate, *Hungry for Life* (Los Angeles: Homeboy Industries, 2013), 43.

10. Norma Mendoza-Denton, *Homegirls: Language and Cultural Practice Among Latina Youth Gangs* (Malden, Mass.: Blackwell, 2008), 90.

11. Mendoza-Denton, 91.

12. Julianne Escobedo Shepherd, "Chola Style: The Latest Cultural Appropriation Fashion Crime?" *Guardian*, August 15, 2014, https://www.theguardian .com/fashion/2014/aug/15/-sp-chola-style-cultural-appropriation-fashion -crime.

13. Rosa Linda Fregoso, "Re-imagining Chicana Urban Identities in the Public Sphere, Cool Chuca Style," in *Between Woman and Nation: Nationalisms, Transnational Feminisms, and the State*, eds. Caren Kaplan, Norma Alarcón, and Minoo Moallem (Durham: Duke University Press, 1999).

14. Quoted in Fregoso, "Re-Imagining Chicana Urban Identities," 79.

15. Tey Diana Rebolledo, *Women Singing in the Snow: A Cultural Analysis of Chicana Literature* (Tucson: University of Arizona Press, 1995), 183.

16. Ofelia Ortiz Cuevas, "Welcome to My Cell: Housing and Race in the Mirror of American Democracy," *American Quarterly* 64 (2012): 605–24.

17. Susana Miyar, "Chocolate Abuelita festeja sus 75 años," *Soy Actitud*, August 20, 2014, http://www.actitudfem.com/hogar/mamas/chocolate-abuelita-festeja-sus-75-anos.

18. Suzanne Chavez-Silverman, "Gendered Bodies and Borders," in *Velvet Barrios: Popular Culture and Chicana/o Sexualities*, ed. Alicia Gaspar de Alba (New York: Palgrave Macmillan, 2003).

19. Isabel Molina Guzmán and Angharad N. Valdivia, "Brain, Brow, and Booty: Latina Iconicity in U.S. Popular Culture," *Communication Review* 7 (2004).

20. Myra Mendible, ed., *From Bananas to Buttocks: The Latina Body in Popular Film and Culture* (Austin: University of Texas Press, 2007), 9–10.

21. Jonathan P. Caulkins and Mark A. R. Kleiman, "Drugs and Crime," in *The Oxford Handbook of Crime and Criminal Justice*, ed. Michael Tonry (New York: Oxford University Press, 2011), 302.

22. Jonathan Xavier Inda, "Foreign Bodies: Migrants, Parasites, and the Pathological Nation," *Discourse* 22, no. 3 (Fall 2000).

23. Daniel Martinez HoSang, *Racial Propositions: Ballot Initiatives and the Making of Postwar California* (Berkeley: University of California Press, 2010), 165.

24. Ann Coulter, *Adios, America: The Left's Plan to Turn Our Country into a Third World Hellhole* (New York: Regnery, 2015), 63.

25. Celeste Fremon, *G-Dog and the Homeboys: Father Greg Boyle and the Gangs of East Los Angeles* (Albuquerque: University of New Mexico Press, 2008).

26. Benét J. Wilson, "The Next Evolution of Airport Dining Is Happening Right Now," Eater, June 28, 2016, https://www.eater.com/2016/6/28/11996892/airport-restaurants-newark-otg.

27. Harriet Baskas, "LAX Homeboy Café Benefits Gang Intervention," Stuck at the Airport, April 16, 2013, http://stuckattheairport.com/2013/04/16/lax-homeboy-cafe-benefits-gang-intervention/.

28. Kate Linthicum, "Homeboy Industries Expands with Diner at City Hall," *Los Angeles Times*, June 11, 2011, http://articles.latimes.com/2011/jun/11/local/la-me-homeboy-city-hall-20110611.

29. "Homeboys Feeding City Hall," *Los Angeles Downtown News*, June 13, 2011, http://www.ladowntownnews.com/news/homeboys-feeding-city-hall/article_b5e627b0-95eb-11e0-9b52-001cc4c002e0.html.

30. Kate Linthicum, "Homeboy Industries Expands with Diner at City Hall," *Los Angeles Times*, http://articles.latimes.com/2011/jun/11/local/la-me-home boy-city-hall-20110611.

31. Ana Elena Puga, "Poor Enrique and Poor María, or The Political Economy of Suffering in Two Migrant Melodramas," in *Performance in the Borderlands*, eds. Ramón H. Rivera-Servera and Harvey Young (New York: Palgrave Macmillan, 2011), 228.

32. Saidiya V. Hartman, *Scenes of Subjection: Terror, Slavery, and Self-Making in Nineteenth-Century America* (Oxford: Oxford University Press, 1997), 21.

33. Anzaldúa, *Borderlands/La Frontera*, 80–81.

Chapter 4

1. The title of this section comes from my son, Emiliano Vargas, who posted a sign that read "The Bean Scene" on his dorm room door when he was a high school student at the Thacher School in Ojai, California. He was playfully proud that his room served as a gathering place for Latinos at an institution where White students were in the majority.

2. Arlene Dávila, *Latinos Inc.: The Marketing and Making of a People* (Berkeley: University of California Press, 2012), 2–3.

3. Catherine M. Tucker, *Coffee Culture: Local Experiences, Global Connections* (New York: Taylor and Francis, 2017), 6.

4. "Coffee: World Markets and Trade," United States Department of Agriculture, accessed June 20, 2017, https://apps.fas.usda.gov/psdonline/circulars /coffee.pdf.

5. "National Coffee Drinking Trends (NCDT) Report," National Coffee Association, December 14, 2017, http://www.ncausa.org/Industry-Resources /Market-Research/National-Coffee-Drinking-Trends-Report#.

6. "Number of Starbucks Stores Worldwide from 2003 to 2017," Statista, accessed December 22, 2017, https://www.statista.com/statistics/266465 /number-of-starbucks-stores-worldwide/.

7. Tucker, *Coffee Culture*, 8.

8. Nicholas Cho, "The BGA and the Third Wave," CoffeeGeek.com, April 1, 2005, http://coffeegeek.com/opinions/bgafiles/04-02-2005/.

9. Timothy Castle, "The Future of Specialty Coffee and the Next Wave," *Coffee Talk*, February 27, 2016, http://coffeetalk.com/ctmagazine/02-2016/24211/.

10. Kim Sheehan, *Controversies in Contemporary Advertising* (Thousand Oaks, Calif.: Sage, 2004), 2–4.

11. Beltrán, *The Trouble with Unity*, 4.

12. Kathleen Franz and Jordan Grant, "Collecting the History of Hispanic Advertising," O Say Can You See? Stories from the National Museum of American History, November 7, 2016, http://americanhistory.si.edu/blog/collecting-history-hispanic-advertising.

13. Gina Grillo, "The Advertising Industry Needs Diverse Leadership to Thrive," AdAge, April 23, 2015, http://adage.com/article/agency-viewpoint/advertising-industry-diverse-leadership-thrive/297998/.

14. "FFF: Hispanic Heritage Month 2016," United States Census Bureau, October 12, 2016, https://www.census.gov/newsroom/facts-for-features/2016/cb16-ff16.html.

15. "Hispanic Influence Reaches New Heights in the U.S.," Nielson, August 23, 2016, http://www.nielsen.com/us/en/insights/news/2016/hispanic-influence-reaches-new-heights-in-the-us.html.

16. Franz and Grant, "Collecting the History."

17. Michèle Lamont and Virág Molnar, "Social Categorization and Group Identification: How African Americans Shape Their Collective Identity Through Consumption," in *Innovation by Demand: An Interdisciplinary Approach to the Study of Demand and its Role in Innovation*, eds. Andrew McMeekin et al. (Manchester: Manchester University Press, 2002), 35.

18. Dávila, *Latinos Inc.*, 25–26.

19. Dávila, *Latinos Inc.*, 105.

20. David Reyes, "Latino Leader Calls for Taco Bell Boycott," *Los Angeles Times*, July 14, 1998, http://articles.latimes.com/1998/jul/14/business/fi-3450.

21. Berg, *Latino Images in Film*, 13–15.

22. Marilyn Kern-Foxworth, *Aunt Jemima, Uncle Ben, And Rastus: Blacks in Advertising, Yesterday, Today, and Tomorrow* (Westport, Conn.: Greenwood Press, 1994), 40–41.

23. Juan Forero, "Medellín Journal: A Coffee Icon Rides His Mule Off into the Sunset," *New York Times*, November 24, 2017, http://www.nytimes.com/2001/11/24/world/medellin-journal-a-coffee-icon-rides-his-mule-off-into-the-sunset.html.

24. Karim León Vargas and Juan Carlos, eds., *Federación Nacional de Café, 1927–2017: 90 años; Vivir el café y sembrar el futuro* (Medellín: Editorial EAFIT, 2017), 12.

25. Vargas and Carlos, *Federación Nacional de Café*, 18.

26. John Cruz, Conversation with the author, October 24, 2017.

27. Laura Kiniry, "Will the Real Juan Valdez Please Stand Up?" Smithsonian.com, September 11, 2011, https://www.smithsonianmag.com/travel/will-the-real -juan-valdez-please-stand-up-68594542/.

28. "Our History," Juan Valdez, accessed December 3, 2017, http://www.juan valdezcafe.com/en-us/our-brand/our-history/.

29. Kiniry, "Will the Real Juan Valdez Please Stand Up?"

30. Quoted in John Isbister, *Promises Not Kept: Poverty and the Betrayal of Third World Development* (Bloomfield, Conn.: Kumarian Press, 2006), 32–41.

31. Isbister, *Promises Not Kept*, 41–48.

32. Linda C. L. Fu, *Advertising and Race: Global Phenomenon, Historical Challenges, and Visual Strategies* (New York: Peter Lang, 2014), 261.

33. Daniel Jaffee, *Brewing Justice: Fair Trade Coffee, Sustainability, and Survival* (Oakland: University of California Press, 2014), 12.

34. Jaffee, *Brewing Justice*, 13.

35. Jonathan Rosenthal, "The Greatest Challenge: Roots of US Fair Trade," in *The Fair Trade Revolution*, ed. John Bowes (New York: Pluto Press, 2011).

36. Jaffee, *Brewing Justice*, 199–31.

37. Keith R. Brown, *Buying into Fair Trade: Culture, Morality, and Consumption* (New York: New York University Press, 2013), 2.

38. Brown, *Buying into Fair Trade*, 5.

39. Jaffee, *Brewing Justice*.

40. United Students for Fair Trade, "United Students for Fair Trade Withdraws Support from Fair Trade USA / Transfair—Calls for Reform to Fair Trade Standards," *Fair World Project*, October 25, 2011, https://fairworldproject .org/united-students-for-fair-trade-withdraws-support-from-fair-trade-usa transfair-calls-for-reform-to-fair-trade-standards/.

41. Pierre Bourdieu, *Distinction: A Social Critique of the Judgment of Good Taste*, trans. Richard Nice (Cambridge, Mass.: Harvard University Press, 1984).

42. Jennifer Tolbert Roberts, *Athens on Trial: The Antidemocratic Tradition in Western Thought* (Princeton: Princeton University Press, 2011), 31.

43. Joel Stein, "Blue Bottle Coffee and the Next Wave of Artisanal Coffee Shops," *Bloomberg*, May 1, 2014, https://www.bloomberg.com/news/articles/2014 -05-01/blue-bottle-coffee-and-the-next-wave-of-artisanal-coffee-shops.

44. Josh Ozersky, "The Perils of Coffee Snobbery: What the Cult of Craft Coffee Says About Our Country," *Time*, September 19, 2012, http://ideas.time.com /2012/09/19/the-perils-of-coffee-snobbery/.

45. "Negative Images 'Brainwash' African Americans," Interview with Tom Burrell, NPR, March 18, 2010, https://www.npr.org/templates/story/story.php?storyId=124828546.

46. "Crossing Over," *AdWeek*, March 21, 2005, http://www.adweek.com/brand-marketing/crossing-over-78436/.

47. Charles R. Taylor and Hue-Kyong Bang, "Portrayals of Latinos in Magazine Advertising," *Journalism & Mass Communication Quarterly* 74, no. 2 (June 1997).

Conclusion

1. Will Dunham, "World's Oceans Clogged by Millions of Tons of Plastic Trash," *Scientific American*, February 12, 2015, https://www.scientificamerican.com/article/world-s-oceans-clogged-by-millions-of-tons-of-plastic-trash/.

2. James Loke Hale, "Why Are Straws So Bad for the Environment? 7 Reasons Cities Are Pushing for Bans," *Bustle*, June 8, 2018, https://www.bustle.com/p/why-are-straws-so-bad-for-the-environment-7-reasons-cities-are-pushing-for-bans-9348478.

3. "Minimizing Food Waste," United Nations Environment Programme, https://www.unenvironment.org/regions/north-america/regional-initiatives/minimizing-food-waste.

4. Joseph Hincks, "The World Is Headed for a Food Security Crisis: Here's How We Can Avert It," *Time*, March 28, 2018, http://time.com/5216532/global-food-security-richard-deverell/.

5. "Food Security Status of U.S. Households in 2016," United States Department of Agriculture Economic Research Service, October 4, 2017, https://www.ers.usda.gov/topics/food-nutrition-assistance/food-security-in-the-us/key-statistics-graphics.aspx.

6. "Gerardo Reyes Chávez of Coalition of Immokalee Workers—Biography," StarChefs, August 2012, https://www.starchefs.com/cook/chefs/bio/gerardo-reyes-chavez.

7. "Half-Way Home," Coalition of Immokalee Workers, June 8, 2018, http://ciw-online.org/blog/2018/06/half-way-home/.

BIBLIOGRAPHY

Abarca, Meredith E., and Nieves Pascual Soler. *Rethinking Chicana/o Literature Through Food: Postnational Appetites*. New York: Palgrave Macmillan, 2013.

Acuña, Rodolfo. *Occupied America: A History of Chicanos*. Uppersaddle River, New Jersey: Pearson, 2015.

Ananth, Akhila L., and Carly B. Dierkhising. *CURE Diversion Program: Process Evaluation Report*. Coalition for Responsible Community Development, 2015.

Anzaldúa, Gloria. *Borderlands / La Frontera: The New Mestiza*. 3rd ed. San Francisco: Aunt Lute Books, 2007.

Arellano, Gustavo. *Taco USA: How Mexican Food Conquered America*. New York: Scribner, 2012.

Barvosa, Edwina. *Wealth of Selves: Multiple Identities, Mestiza Consciousness, and the Subject of Politics*. College Station: Texas A&M University Press, 2008.

Batalla, Guillermo Bonfil. *México Profundo: Reclaiming a Civilization*. Translated by Philip Adams Dennis. Austin: University of Texas Press, 1996.

Beltrán, Cristina. *The Trouble with Unity: Latino Politics and the Creation of Identity*. Oxford: Oxford University Press, 2010.

Berg, Charles Ramírez. *Latino Images in Film: Stereotypes, Subversion, and Resistance*. Austin: University of Texas Press, 2002.

Bourdieu, Pierre. *Distinction: A Social Critique of the Judgment of Good Taste*. Translated by Richard Nice. Cambridge, Mass.: Harvard University Press, 1984.

Boyle, Gregory. *Tattoos on the Heart: The Power of Boundless Compassion*. New York: Free Press, 2010.

Brown, Keith R. *Buying into Fair Trade: Culture, Morality, and Consumption*. New York: New York University Press, 2013.

Burciaga, José Antonio. *Undocumented Love / Amor Indocumentado*. San Jose: Chusma House, 1992.

Calvo, Luz, and Catriona Rueda Esquibel. *Plant-Based Mexican-American Recipes for Health and Healing*. Vancouver: Arsenal Pulp Press, 2015.

Caulkins, Jonathan P., and Mark A. R. Kleiman. "Drugs and Crime." In *The Oxford Handbook of Crime and Criminal Justice*, edited by Michael Tonry, 275–320. New York: Oxford University Press, 2011.

Cepeda, Maria Elena. "'Columbus Effect(s)': Chronology and Crossover in the Latin(o) Music 'Boom.'" *Discourse* 23, no. 1 (2001): 62–81.

Chabrán, Rafael. "Dr. Francisco Hernandez Ate Tacos: The Food and Drinks of the Mexican Treasury." *Diálogo: An Interdisciplinary Studies Journal* 18, no. 1 (2015): 19–32.

Chavez-Silverman, Suzanne. "Gendered Bodies and Borders." In *Velvet Barrios: Popular Culture and Chicana/o Sexualities*, edited by Alicia Gaspar de Alba, 215–27. New York: Palgrave Macmillan, 2003.

Cobb, Russell, ed. *The Paradox of Authenticity in a Globalized World*. New York: Palgrave Macmillan, 2014.

Contreras, Sheila. *Blood Lines: Myth, Indigenism, and Chicana/o Literature*. Austin: University of Texas Press, 2008.

Coulter, Ann, *Adios, America: The Left's Plan to Turn Our Country into a Third World Hellhole*. New York: Regnery, 2015.

Dávila, Arlene. *Latinos Inc.: The Marketing and Making of a People*. Berkeley: University of California Press, 2012.

Davis, Angela. *Are Prisons Obsolete?* New York: Seven Stories Press, 2003.

Davis, Angela. "The Prison Industrial Complex." In *Civil Rights Since 1787: A Reader on the Black Struggle*, edited by Jonathan Birnbaum and Clarence Taylor, 823–28. New York: New York University Press, 2000.

Esquivel, Laura. *Como agua para chocolate*. New York: Anchor Books, 1989.

Faber, Daniel. *The Struggle for Ecological Democracy: Environmental Justice Movements in the United States*. London: Guilford Press, 1998.

Fitting, Elizabeth. "Cultures of Corn and Anti-GMO Activism in Mexico and Columbia." In *Food Activism: Agency, Democracy and Economy*, edited by Carole Counihan and Valeria Siniscalchi, 175–92. New York: Bloomsbury, 2014.

Fonseca, Vanessa. "Fractal Capitalism and the Latinization of the US Market." PhD diss., University of Texas at Austin, 2003.

Fregoso, Rosa Linda. "Re-imagining Chicana Urban Identities in the Public Sphere, Cool Chuca Style." In *Between Woman and Nation: Nationalisms, Transnational Feminisms, and the State*, edited by Caren Kaplan, Norma Alarcón, and Minoo Moallem, 72–91. Durham: Duke University Press, 1999.

Fremon, Celeste. *G-Dog and the Homeboys: Father Greg Boyle and the Gangs of East Los Angeles*. Albuquerque: University of New Mexico Press, 2008.

Fu, Linda C. L. *Advertising and Race: Global Phenomenon, Historical Challenges, and Visual Strategies*. New York: Peter Lang, 2014.

Giagnoni, Silvia. *Fields of Resistance*. Chicago: Haymarket Books, 2011.

Gonzalez, Juan. *Harvest of Empire: A History of Latinos in America*. New York: Penguin Books, 2011.

Gonzalez, Juan Carlos, and Edwardo Portillos. "The Undereducation and Overcriminalization of U.S. Latinas/os: A Post–Los Angeles Riots LatCrit Analysis." *Educational Studies* 42, no. 3 (2007): 247–66.

Goodman, David, E. Melanie DuPuis, and Michael K. Goodman. *Alternative Food Networks: Knowledge, Practice, and Politics*. New York: Routledge, 2012.

Guthman, Julie. *The Paradox of Organic Farming in California*. 2nd ed. Oakland: University of California Press, 2014.

Guzmán, Isabel Molina, and Angharad N. Valdivia. "Brain, Brow, and Booty: Latina Iconicity in U.S. Popular Culture." *Communication Review* 7 (2004): 205–21.

Hartman, Saidiya V. *Scenes of Subjection: Terror, Slavery, and Self-Making in Nineteenth-Century America*. Oxford: Oxford University Press, 1997.

Hernandez, Deborah Pacini. *Oye Como Va! Hybridity and Identity in Latin American Popular Music*. Philadelphia: Temple University Press, 2010.

Hernández, Kelly Lytle. "The Crimes and Consequences of Illegal Immigration: A Cross-Border Examination of Operation Wetback, 1943 to 1954." *Western Historical Quarterly* 37 (Winter 2006): 421–44.

Holmes, Seth. *Fresh Fruit, Broken Bodies: Migrant Farmworkers in the United States*. Berkeley: University of California Press, 2013.

HoSang, Daniel Martinez. *Racial Propositions: Ballot Initiatives and the Making of Postwar California*. Berkeley: University of California Press, 2010.

Inda, Jonathan Xavier. "Foreign Bodies: Migrants, Parasites, and the Pathological Nation." *Discourse* 22, no. 3 (Fall 2000): 46–62.

Irazábal, Clara, and Ramzi Farhat. "Latino Communities in the United States: Place-Making in the Pre–World War II, Postwar, and Contemporary City." *Journal of Planning Literature* 22, no. 3 (2008): 207–28.

Isbister, John. *Promises Not Kept: Poverty and the Betrayal of Third World Development.* Bloomfield, Conn.: Kumarian Press, 2006.

Jaffee, Daniel. *Brewing Justice: Fair Trade Coffee, Sustainability, and Survival.* Oakland: University of California Press, 2014.

Janer, Zilkia. *Latino Food Culture.* Westport, Conn.: Greenwood Press, 2008.

Johnston, Josée, and Shyon Baumann. *Foodies: Democracy and Distinction in the Gourmet Foodscape.* New York: Routledge, 2010.

Kaplan, Caren, Norma Alarcón, and Minoo Moallem. *Between Woman and Nation: Nationalisms, Transnational Feminisms, and the State.* Durham. Duke University Press, 1999.

Kern-Foxworth, Marilyn. *Aunt Jemima, Uncle Ben, and Rastus: Blacks in Advertising, Yesterday, Today, and Tomorrow.* Westport, Conn.: Greenwood Press, 1994.

Lamont, Michèle, and Virág Molnár, "Social Categorization and Group Identification: How African Americans Shape Their Collective Identity Through Consumption." In *Innovation by Demand: An Interdisciplinary Approach to the Study of Demand and its Role in Innovation,* edited by Andrew McMeekin, Mark Tomlinson, Ken Green, Vivien Walsh, 88–111. Manchester: Manchester University Press, 2002.

Lockhart, James. *Nahuatl as Written: Lessons in Older Written Nahuatl, with Copious Examples and Texts.* Stanford: Stanford University Press and UCLA Latin American Studies, 2001.

Lopez-Aguado, Patrick. "The Collateral Consequences of Prisonization: Racial Sorting, Carceral Identity, and Community Criminalization." *Sociology Compass* 10, no. 1 (January 2016): 12–23.

Martinez-Cruz, Paloma. *Women and Knowledge in Mesoamerica: From East L.A. to Anahuac.* Tucson: University of Arizona Press, 2011.

Martinez Pompa, Paul. *My Kill Adore Him.* Notre Dame: University of Notre Dame Press, 2009.

McFarland, Louis. *The Chican@ Hip Hop Nation.* East Lansing: Michigan State University Press, 2013.

McNamee, Thomas, Alice Waters, and Chez Panisse. *The Romantic, Impractical, Often Eccentric, Ultimately Brilliant Making of a Food Revolution.* New York: Penguin Press, 2007.

Mendible, Myra, ed. *From Bananas to Buttocks: The Latina Body in Popular Film and Culture.* Austin: University of Texas Press, 2007.

Mendoza-Denton, Norma. *Homegirls: Language and Cultural Practice Among Latina Youth Gangs.* Malden, Mass.: Blackwell, 2008.

Mignolo, Walter. *The Darker Side of Western Modernity: Global Futures, Decolonial Options.* Durham: Duke University Press, 2011.

Miranda, Marie "Keta." *Homegirls in the Public Sphere.* Austin: University of Texas Press, 2003.

Moloney, Molly, Geoffrey Hunt, Karen Joe-Laidler, and Kathleen MacKenzie. "Young Mother (in the) Hood: Gang Girls' Negotiation of New Identities." *Journal of Youth Studies* 14, no. 1 (2011): 1–19.

Moore, Lorie, and Irene Padavic. "Racial and Ethnic Disparities in Girls' Sentencing in the Juvenile Justice System." *Feminist Criminology* 5, no. 3 (2010): 263–85.

Morgan, Kevin, Terry Marsden, and Jonathan Murdoch. *Worlds of Food: Place, Power, and Provenance in the Food Chain.* New York: Oxford University Press, 2006.

Murray, Zachiah. *Mindfulness in the Garden: Zen Tools for Digging in the Dirt.* Berkeley: Parallax Press, 2012.

Ochoa, Enrique C. "From Tortillas to Low-Carb Capitalism and Mexican Food in Los Angeles Since the 1920s." *Diálogo: An Interdisciplinary Studies Journal* 18, no. 1 (2015): 33–46.

Ontiveros, Randy. *In the Spirit of a New People: The Cultural Politics of the Chicano Movement*. New York: New York University Press, 2013.

Ortiz Cuevas, Ofelia. "Welcome to My Cell: Housing and Race in the Mirror of American Democracy." *American Quarterly* 64 (2012): 605–24.

Peña, Devon G. *Mexican Americans and the Environment: Tierra y Vida*. Tucson: University of Arizona Press, 2005.

Pérez-Torres, Rafael. *Mestizaje: Critical Uses of Race in Chicano Culture*. Minneapolis: University of Minnesota Press, 2006.

Pilcher, Jeffrey. *Planet Taco: A Global History of Mexican Food*. Oxford: Oxford University Press, 2012.

Pilcher, Jeffrey. *Que vivan los tamales!* Albuquerque: University of New Mexico Press, 1998.

Pinedo, Encarnación. *Encarnación's Kitchen: Mexican Recipes from Nineteenth-Century California*. Translated by Dan Strehl. Berkeley: University of California Press, 2005.

Pratt, Mary Louise. *Imperial Eyes: Travel Writing and Transculturation*. New York: Taylor and Francis, 1992.

Puga, Ana Elena. "Poor Enrique and Poor María, or the Political Economy of Suffering in Two Migrant Melodramas." In *Performance in the Borderlands*, edited by Ramón H. Rivera-Servera and Harvey Young, 225–47. New York: Palgrave Macmillan, 2011.

Pulido, Laura. *Environmentalism and Economic Justice: Two Chicano Struggles in the Southwest*. Tucson: University of Arizona Press, 1996.

Quicker, John C. *Homegirls: Characterizing Chicana Gangs*. San Pedro, Calif.: International Universities Press, 1983.

Quijano, Anibal. "Coloniality of Power, Eurocentrism and Latin America." *Nepantla: Views from South* 1, no. 3 (2000): 533–80.

Quintana, Alvina. *Homegirls: Chicana Literary Voices*. Philadelphia: Temple University Press, 1996.

Rebolledo, Tey Diana. *Women Singing in the Snow: A Cultural Analysis of Chicana Literature*. Tucson: University of Arizona Press, 1995.

Rios, Victor M., and Patrick Lopez-Aguado. "'Pelones y Matones': Chicano Cholos Perform for a Punitive Audience." In *Performing the U.S. Latina and Latino Borderlands*, edited by Arturo J. Aldama, Chela Sandoval, and Peter J. García, 382–401. Bloomington: Indiana University Press, 2012.

Roberts, Jennifer Tolbert. *Athens on Trial: The Antidemocratic Tradition in Western Thought*. Princeton: Princeton University Press, 2011.

Rodriguez, Roberto Cintli. *Our Sacred Maíz Is Our Mother: Indigeneity and Belonging in the Americas*. Tucson: University of Arizona Press, 2014.

Rosenthal, Jonathan. "The Greatest Challenge: Roots of US Fair Trade." In *The Fair Trade Revolution*, edited by John Bowes, 157–72. New York: Pluto Press, 2011.

Saldaña-Portillo, Josefina. "Who's the Indian in Aztlán? Re-writing Mestizaje, Indianism, and Chicanismo from the Lacandón." In *The Latin American Subaltern Studies Reader*, edited by Ileana Rodríguez, 402–23. Durham: Duke University Press, 2001.

Saldivar-Hull, Sonia. "Feminism on the Border: From Gender Politics to Geopolitics." In *Criticism in the Borderlands: Studies in Chicano Literature, Culture and Ideology*, edited by Hector Calderon and Jose David Saldivar, 203–21. Durham: Duke University Press, 1991.

Sánchez, Rosaura. *Chicano Discourse: Socio-Historic Perspectives*. Houston: Arte Público Press, 1983.

Sandoval, Chela. "Mestizaje as Method: Feminists-of-Color Challenge the Canon." In *Living Chicana Theory*, edited by Carla Trujillo, 532–70. Berkeley: Third Woman Press, 1998.

Schumacher, Michael Allen, and Gwen A. Kurz. *The 8% Solution: Preventing Serious, Repeat Juvenile Crime*. Thousand Oaks, Calif.: Sage, 2000.

Segura, Denise A., and Beatriz M. Pesquera. "Beyond Indifference and Antipathy: The Chicana Movement and Chicana Feminist Discourse." *Aztlán Journal* 19, no. 2 (1992): 69–93.

Sheehan, Kim. *Controversies in Contemporary Advertising.* Thousand Oaks, Calif.: Sage, 2004.

Smith, Linda Tuhiwai. *Decolonizing Methodologies: Research and Indigenous Peoples.* London: Zed Books, 2002.

Soldatenko, Michael. "Tacos and Coloniality: A Review Essay." *Diálogo: An Interdisciplinary Studies Journal* 18, no. 1 (2015): 135–42.

Stavans, Ilán. *Mexican-American Cuisine.* Santa Barbara, Calif.: Greenwood, 2011.

Sussman, Rachel. "The Carnavalizing of Race." *Etnofoor* 14, no. 2 (2001): 79–88.

Taylor, Charles R., and Hue-Kyong Bang. "Portrayals of Latinos in Magazine Advertising." *Journalism and Mass Communication Quarterly* 74, no. 2 (June 1997): 285–303.

Trouillot, Michel-Rolph. *Silencing the Past: Power and the Production of History.* Boston: Beacon Press, 2015.

Tucker, Catherine M. *Coffee Culture: Local Experiences, Global Connections.* New York: Taylor and Francis, 2017.

Varga, Joseph J. "Breaking the Heartland: Creating the Precariat in the US Lower Rust Belt." *Global Discourse: An Interdisciplinary Journal of Current Affairs and Applied Contemporary Thought* 3, nos. 3–4 (2013): 430–46.

Vargas, Karim León, and Juan Carlos, eds. *Federación Nacional de Café, 1927–2017: 90 años; Vivir el café y sembrar el futuro.* Medellín: Editorial EAFIT, 2017.

Vigil, James Diego. "Group Processes and Street Identity: Adolescent Chicano Gang Members." *Ethos* 16, no. 4 (1988): 421–45.

Vilchis, Jaime. "¿Qué comía Dr. Francisco Hernández (1517–1578)? La intermediación de mestizaje y gastronómica del Protomédico de Indias de Felipe II." *Diálogo: An Interdisciplinary Studies Journal* 18, no. 1 (2015): 5–17.

Wade, Peter, Carlos López Beltrán, Eduardo Restrepo, and Ricardo Ventura Santos, eds. *Mestizo Genomics: Race Mixture, Nation, and Science in Latin America.* Durham, Duke University Press, 2014.

Warde, Alan. *Consumption, Food, and Taste.* London: Sage, 1997.

Young, Robert J. C. *Colonial Desire: Hybridity, Culture and Race.* New York: Routledge, 1995.

Zarate, Pati. *Hungry for Life.* Los Angeles: Homeboy Industries, 2013.

Zatz, Marjorie, and Edwardo L. Portillos. "Voices from the Barrio: Chicano/a Gangs, Families, and Communities." *Criminology* 38, no. 2 (2000): 369–402.

INDEX

ABOUT THE AUTHOR

PALOMA MARTINEZ-CRUZ is an associate professor of Latinx cultural studies at The Ohio State University. She is the author of *Women and Knowledge in Mesoamerica: From East L.A. to Anahuac.*